Spiritual Direction for Every Christian

SPIRITUAL DIRECTION FOR EVERY CHRISTIAN

Gordon H. Jeff

First published in Great Britain 1987
SPCK
Holy Trinity Church
Marylebone Road
London NW1 4DU

Second impression 1989

British Library Cataloguing in Publication Data

Jeff, Gordon H.
    Spiritual direction
    for every christian.
    1. Pastoral counselling
    I. Title
    253.5   BV4012.2

ISBN 0-281-04318-3

Photoset in Great Britain by
Rowland Phototypesetting Ltd, Bury St Edmunds, Suffolk
and printed by St Edmundsbury Press Ltd
Bury St Edmunds, Suffolk

Contents

Acknowledgements

I am deeply grateful to all my friends in the parish of Carshalton Beeches, where it has been my privilege to minister for the past seven years, for putting up with the working out of this approach to parochial ministry. It has not been what many of them expected, but I truly believe the Holy Spirit has been at work in our midst.

Small though this book may be it would not have been possible without help, in particular from all who have given me the privilege of being a spiritual friend to them, from Alan Harrison, my own director, and from my colleague Dorothy Nicholson who has been responsible as much as I for developing the experimental retreat work and now shares with me in organizing the courses in spiritual direction.

Without Derek Blows' intervention eight years ago, the whole SPIDIR project in the Diocese of Southwark would have died at birth, and without Judy Spolton's careful typing the manuscript would have remained illegible.

Last but not least I am grateful to Colette, my wife, for coping as always so valiantly with half the book being written on holiday and the other half while we were changing both houses and jobs.

1 Elitism or a Path for All?

It all depends on where you are.

In a perfect world, perhaps it would not happen, but fashions affect church life just as they affect any other area of life. There is always an 'in' thing, always something just becoming an 'in' thing and always something which many look at sniffily as rather old hat.

What sort of thing has been in fashion in Christian circles? Christian Stewardship? Small group work? Pastoral counselling? Church growth? Experiential learning? Ministry of healing? Management techniques? Meditation and contemplation? Charismatic gifts? Work supervision? Parish auditing?

Yet what may seem old hat to those at the centre of things may in many parishes have hardly been heard of. It must be the experience of countless parish priests to move into a new parish innocently assuming that the people there are surely familiar with, say, something as long-established as small group work, or shared ministry, or widely accepted liturgical reform – only to find storms and tempests raging around their heads because all this is totally fresh to people, and therefore alarming.

So with spiritual direction. If publishers' lists are anything to go by, spiritual direction is a fashionable growth industry; but ask many good practising Christians about spiritual direction and you will receive a blank look, or the response that whatever it is, it's not for them. Maybe for their vicar, but even there I am not sure. One person who came to me recently from a major parish had asked about spiritual direction and was told by the incumbent that this was something very unusual, and that in a lifetime's ministry he had only come across two people who had had a spiritual director.

I have written this little book, not in any vain attempt to rival the important writing of such people as Kenneth Leech or Christopher Bryant[1] in this country, or the cornucopia of frequently very good books currently arriving from the United States, but to try to carry an awareness of the value of spiritual direction into some of the places other books may not have

1

reached. This is unashamedly a book aimed at any interested person, and I shall try not to take anything for granted, even if this means some readers may at times be traversing familiar ground. As a busy parish priest for the last quarter of a century I shall be writing very much from experience, and to some extent this book is my own story of slow learning from sizeable failures and small successes. It makes no claim to be other than a simple introduction.

I can only hope that my own experience may echo that of other clergy and laity, and may possibly help others to evolve more quickly than I did what at last seems to be a really worthwhile ministry, devoted primarily to some of the things which matter most.

Who's for spiritual direction?

When one hears someone described as a spiritual director, one might, at least subconsciously, picture an ageless, emaciated man in a cowled robe, with eyes cast down and his hands hidden in flowing sleeves. He sits in a whitewashed, cramped room with one small, barred window high on the wall beside him. Opposite him, wearing dun-coloured travelling-dress and bonnet, sits a seventeenth-century French lady. Between them is a table on which rest a skull and a guttered candle. She is describing the miseries of managing the family estate with her husband away at Court for much of the year. He is murmuring about being alone with the Alone, or dictating an horarium that will enable her to bring a measure of monastic order and piety into her life.[2]

This may well be only an entertaining fantasy but it has an element of truth about it. Spiritual direction (we shall try to define it more closely later) is all too often thought of as a self-indulgent luxury for the specially elite – monks and nuns, some clergy, the leisured intelligentsia. It carries with it an aura of escape from real life into some disembodied 'spiritual' world. Somewhere in the background hangs a sinister whiff of authoritarianism, with one person under the thumb of another person who tells them in their great wisdom what to do, or more probably what *not* to do.

More true to life, yet still sad, is that image of a tiny number of very holy men (surprisingly, one or two special women seem also to have been admitted) like 'Father X', to whom 'everybody goes', who is 'very good at direction'.

This elitist view of spiritual direction has done immeasurable harm, and has inhibited many Christians from going to talk through where they are with some understanding person. It is a view reinforced by such alarming observations as that of St John of the Cross, who in writing of spiritual directors commented tartly: 'Not one in a thousand is capable', amended later by St Francis de Sales to 'Not one in ten thousand'. We shall see as we proceed why directors have had such a bad press, but even in our own day this elitist view receives confirmation from such a book as the late Martin Thornton's *Spiritual Direction*.[3] This is in many respects a very good book, but it leaves the reader with the impression that, on the basis of Thornton's rigorous standards, there might well be no more than half a dozen people in any diocese who would come up to scratch.

We have thus reached an early parting of the ways. Either spiritual directors are a very rare, almost extinct breed, and therefore there must be two classes of Christian. On the one hand are a tiny number of the elite who need or will benefit from spiritual direction; on the other hand the great mass of Christians for whom there are not enough spiritual directors to go round and who must perforce cope without.

Or, and this is the basic assumption on which this book is founded, *some kind* of spiritual direction is helpful for every Christian person. If this be so, then since the good Lord would not have created such a need without the possibility of its being met, there must exist a considerable reservoir of listening, spiritually receptive people, lay or ordained, women or men, whose sensitivity can be developed with suitable training and support. If some kind of spiritual direction is appropriate for all Christians, then some of the great mystique as well as all of the bad old authoritarianism has got to go, and we are into something much more low key.

I am aware that I am here apparently taking issue with as eminent a writer as Thomas Merton, who writes: 'Strictly speaking, spiritual direction is not necessary for the ordinary Christian.' He continues, 'Wherever there is *special mission or vocation* a certain minimum of direction is implied by the very nature of the vocation itself.'[4]

It needs to be borne in mind, however, that not only is this relatively early writing from Merton, but he takes for granted a regular meeting of the 'ordinary Christian' (I am not happy with Merton's term!) with his or her confessor. He goes on to say, 'Even ordinary confessions should involve some spiritual direction. It is very unfortunate that many busy priests have come to forget or neglect this obligation.' If I read Merton aright, he is really arguing, as I am doing, that *every* Christain will benefit from some measure of direction.

Starting from where people are

Forget for a while, if you will, the question of regular meetings with a director, and also, for a while, the distinctions between clinical, problem-solving models and healthy growth models. Forget, for a while, the differences between counselling and direction, between teaching and support, between reinforcement and non-directiveness. Let us start where people are.

A Christian person has a decision to make about a job, a training course, a relationship. There are many angles to be looked at in each case, but overarching all of these practical aspects lies the prior question for every Christian, 'What does *God* want me to do?'. That underlying question brings us immediately into the ambience of spiritual direction, even though we may hesitate to use so grand a term. That person may well talk through the issue with someone who may totally leave out the dimension of God. It would surely be better if they could find a member of their church who had some sensitivity in helping them to discern where God's path for them might lie, while not neglecting all the practical details of the decision.

Some may not even consider this kind of situation as coming under the heading of spiritual direction – this humble, humdrum, ordinary everyday scenario. But one such decision may alter the whole of a person's life, and it is reasonable that every Christian should feel there is someone they can turn to, not so as to be told what to do nor to make them childishly dependent, but with whom they can learn to be more open to the guidance of the Holy Spirit. Clearly, that saintly Father X, to whom everybody who is anybody goes for spiritual direction, will not have time for a situation like this multiplied thousands of times across a diocese.

Take a second basic situation; a Christian reaches some kind of turning point in life, or something brings them to realize the time may have come to take their relationship with God more seriously. An encounter, a sermon, a group experience, or even one of those much-maligned Stewardship campaigns may have prompted them to want to talk: 'Where am I up to in my prayer life, my work, my family, in relation to God?' It may be years since they sat down with someone else and looked at themselves before God. Perhaps they have never before talked seriously with anyone about their life in relationship to God. I find it a never-ending source of dismay how many Christians, maybe churchgoers for years, have never seriously sat down and talked through where their lives are up to and where they are going in relationship with God, about how their prayer life is developing, or about where God has been at work in their everyday world.

But if any such person finds a responsive and sympathetic ear, it is likely that (again without creating dependency) they will want this talking through to become a regular meeting – a kind of stocktaking. Not because they have any particular problems, but to help them to grow more effectively and make the most of all the potentialities and gifts God has given them.

At this point, we are moving towards making some kind of a contract – would it be helpful for them to come and talk a couple of times a year? Or quarterly? Or if a new pattern of prayer and growing awareness of God is being established, perhaps monthly for a short while?

Clearly what we are talking about has nothing to do with interminable psychotherapy, but with relatively infrequent meetings which often enable real spiritual friendship to develop over a period of time, and which by nature of the infrequency allow a director to be in touch with a relatively large number of people.

Is it totally unrealistic to suggest that every single Christian would benefit from talking over – even if only once a year – how they were getting on in their Christian pilgrimage, and especially in their direct relationship with God which we call prayer?

After all, in any secular *work* situation we talk through where we are up to; in any secular *learning* situation we talk through where we are up to. It seems to me more and more absurd that Christians should go through their lives without a regular stock-taking and raising of potentialities and difficulties with someone who has had the experience and privilege of observing the spiritual journeys of others. People so often worry about what are in fact common difficulties shared by most of us; or a mistaken understanding of some aspect of Christian teaching may be adversely affecting their lives. Just as a simple visit to our doctor may be all that is needed to reassure us about a medical matter, so in many instances someone to turn to on a spiritual matter may be all that is needed to release new activities and new growth.

But to whom do we go?

If that wonderful Father X. seems too exalted for my beginner's situation, to whom do I turn?

The Vicar? Poor man, he never seems to have a minute to spare, dashing from committee to synod, to chapter meeting, to fraternal, to organizations and planning meetings. His diary seems to be full for the next month, with finance committees and those high-powered diocesan activities he seems to enjoy more than his work in the parish. And even when I corner him, he seems embarrassed to talk about God and about the other things that really matter to me.

Unfair to Vicars? Maybe. Maybe what they are really longing for is that more people *would* come and talk to them about God, but they manage to give such an impression of busy-ness that people are reluctant to burden them further with matters of prayer which may not appear to be urgent. Some clergy have a need to feel wanted, and therefore cultivate this impression of hectic busy-ness. Times without number people who have come to me have said, 'I couldn't possibly have talked with my own vicar about all these things.' This may or may not be true, since sometimes they appear not to have tried, but we shall look in the last chapter at whether this obsessive busy-ness is the best way to run a parish, and whether it is really necessary to be so busy.

So where to turn? In all probability the person who wants to find someone to talk to simply shuts up and talks with nobody. There is no-one obvious to turn to. In most congregations or Christian communities, however, there are several wise lay-people to whom others quietly go to talk and share their concerns. Probably they will have no official accreditation or formal theological training, and may even go virtually unrecognized. But they are there. They may quietly come into their own at prayer groups in the discussion over coffee which usually follows the praying (we shall look at that later, too).

Here, I believe, lies the potential in each community for spiritual direction, as well as by finding ways of freeing the clergy from their obsession with organizations so as to allow them more time to help individuals grow in their Christian life. If we can only lose the elitist mystique, and simply think of John or Mary talking with another Christian person about their relationship to God (or about their lack of any experience of God), then I think we are on the right road. There is a pressing need to train future spiritual directors in some depth, and this is an increasing part of my own ministry; but we can start in a humble way with people who are already used, whose gifts can be developed. I can see no future, however, in running courses for people who are not already perceived by others to have the right kind of sensitivity or to have experienced (and perhaps overcome) problems and uncertainties like their own. Mere completion of a course will not make a spiritual director, but I believe we can build on gifts and experience already perceived and used.

Developing the ability to direct

I don't know how far my own story is shared by other clergy, and I may be a slow developer, but it has seemed to me that while there may be a sprinkling of younger men and women who are used as spiritual directors, in general it is only as we gain some measure of maturity that people come to us for direction. I can even detect a kind of progression; as a young curate people tended to ask me practical, secular, 'Citizen's Advice Bureau' questions, about housing and benefits and social security. As time went on, however, the number of personal and emotional problems coming my way led me to train and work as a marriage guidance counsellor, and to go through Clinical Theology training and extended training and practice in group counselling.

My counselling period lasted a good number of years, but the way things were set up made it difficult in group work to address oneself to the underlying God-questions, and during a period as a rural dean I realized that a significant number of clergy were coming to talk with me not only about pastoral questions, but about deeper things, about difficulties in prayer, doubts and loss of faith.

Perhaps those questions had been put before me all the time in veiled form and I had simply been deaf to them because of the psychological counselling stance I had been taking; but it seemed that gradually I was being approached more frequently about prayer and the relationship of work and family life to God. There was nothing of the ivory tower about what was increasingly coming my way.

It was largely my own fault that I was so slow in developing. For years I had been lazy about finding a director for myself, perhaps partly because I had plenty of support in my counselling work. From time to time I would talk through where I stood with God with anyone around who seemed able to hear, but for a long while had no regular director. So what conceivable right had I – it now seems so clear – to expect anyone to come to talk to me about their spiritual path, when I was not prepared to go along the sometimes painful road of sharing my own spiritual develop-ment with someone else? St Thomas Aquinas put it bluntly: 'He who makes himself his own teacher becomes the pupil of a fool'.

I cannot stress too strongly that if we are to be any good with others we need to be under direction ourselves. My guess is that many clergy who complain that no one comes to talk with them do not themselves take their own deepest concerns to anyone else.

I was brought up in a tradition which did not advocate sacramental confession, and for years again I was very lax about confession. Yet here the same principle applies: it cannot be right to hear the confessions of others unless we are ready to place ourselves in the humble position of the penitent. We shall look later at how confession and spiritual direction are related to each other, but for the moment I simply wish to underline the points already made. If we expect to be used as directors we need to be under direction ourselves (and if priests hearing the confessions of others, to be making our own confessions). And if we are involved in parochial work we need to find ways of showing that we have p'enty of time to spare for people who may be hesitant to think they are even 'worth' our time, or that their concerns are sufficiently 'important'.

Finally, and maybe much more difficult – learning to let go of personal ambition for visible 'success' either in a parish or in secular work, along with refraining from over-involvement in diocesan and other extra-parochial concerns is a pretty good starting point for serving people as a spiritual director.

2 What are People's Needs?

Before attempting to consider different kinds of spiritual direction it would seem sensible to look a little more closely at what are the needs. There are the overt needs and there are the potential openings:

'Can you recommend someone as a spiritual director?' or

'I've been looking around for ages for a director and can't find anyone who seems to fulfil what I'm looking for.'

Whether or not because of the current fashionableness of spiritual direction, I seem to be meeting remarks like these more and more frequently. In many dioceses, and on many training courses, participants are being strongly recommended to have a director, but those who ask trainees to find a director do not have very appropriate suggestions to make about who to go to.

In SPIDIR – a network in the Diocese of Southwark for all who are interested in spiritual direction, and for setting up training courses in spiritual direction (I shall be writing about this organization in more detail in Chapter 9) – we have always declined to maintain a list of 'spiritual directors'. It is hard to set up criteria to determine who would be effective; some who are excellent could well be left off the list, and without knowing something about both director and potential client one needs to be wary about assessing suitability and 'matching up'. Where we have received specific individual requests for a director, committee members have tried to make suggestions from their own personal knowledge. For some years I have been on a list of directors for the Julian meetings, who *do* keep a list, but it may be significant that I have not had a single request for help from this source. As things stand at the moment, there frequently seems to be little other to do than offer the advice which has been standard for years: 'Keep on asking around in your part of the world till you find out who are the people others go to.'

The straight request for a spiritual director may sometimes conceal a background in which an earlier director has been found unhelpful, or in which the directee has simply grown out of an existing director. When St John of the Cross and Francis de Sales inveighed against bad directors they were almost certainly complaining about over-directiveness. It cannot be said too often and too firmly that the only true director is the Holy Spirit. Direction, as I understand it, is two people sitting down together in an attitude of prayer to try to discern where the Holy Spirit is directing. The 'director', from his or her experience of others, from insight or wisdom, may sometimes have suggestions to offer to the 'directee'; but the whole exercise is one in which the potential of the directee is being helped to emerge, and not in any sense a pushing of directees into any one kind of path of prayer. The role of the director is much more that of the person who asks important questions which may not have been considered, and leaves the directee to find out his or her own answers. All too many people have come to me unhappily from directors who themselves stood too firmly in one particular spiritual tradition and tried to push clients on to their own particular path, instead of helping them to grow into the unique individuals they have it in themselves, under God, to become.

I think we can go further: not only are some pushed into traditions of spirituality unsuitable for them or unsuitable for where they are at a particular stage of their journey, but an increasing number of people have had some experience of being counselled, usually in a non-directive way, and have come to expect the freedom and the time to talk quite widely and unconstrainedly where they are. What may appear on the surface to be a question of prayer may well be a question of relationships, but this needs a generous gift of time to uncover, and an older tradition of spiritual direction may simply not allow sufficient time, nor adequately wide-ranging discussion for the deeper aspects of people's concerns to be uncovered.

So at the level of *overt* needs in direction we have those who are looking quite simply for someone to 'take them on', and some of these may well be wanting a change either because of their present director's unsuitability or over-directiveness, or because of their own growth, or the need to be given more time and 'space'.

The next area where an adequate supply of competent directors is needed is shown by the bewilderment so often expressed about how to pray. The question raised by the anonymous pilgrim in *The Way of a Pilgrim* remains as searching a one today as when he raised it. Everyone told him he *ought* to pray, but no-one told him *how* to pray, and the book is the story of his search for the answer to that question. There are countless books around these days on how to pray; indeed, far too many. But it is significant that the Pilgrim found his answer not in widely addressed sermons or teaching, but in one-to-one discussion with others. In other words, the teaching he received was appropriate for what he needed at that particular time. He needed individual spiritual direction.

In the absence of directors a majority of people may well have to find their own way in prayer from reading books; but again, with notable exceptions, too many books on prayer offer us enthusiastic advice on how to follow one particular tradition of prayer which may be excellent for the person who wrote the book, but not necessarily helpful for the person who reads it. Many have given up the serious attempt to pray because they have tried to follow inappropriate paths in prayer. There is all the difference in the world between the pattern of prayer that suits a person who responds primarily in a *thinking* manner and one that suits someone who works primarily in a *feeling* manner, just as there is a real difference in prayer needs between those who find words come alive for them and those who respond more readily to visual symbols. Faced with such wide variations of temperament, surely it is not expecting too much to have a vision of a church where each member goes along, if only once or twice a year, to talk over with someone else how their prayer life is getting on.

Books are also discouraging to many who feel their prayer life is almost non-existent. I sometimes feel that prayer can all too easily become just another item in a long list of possible self-improvement exercises, all needing half an hour a day (yoga, jogging, prayer, relaxation, serious reading, gardening, journal-keeping, etc., etc., etc.,) so that there is nothing left of the day for anything *but* self-improvement!

By talking on a one-to-one basis from time to time, beginners on the path of prayer can be encouraged onwards from where they are, and often helped to realize that they are already effectively praying when they don't think they are. In other words, prayer is a much wider activity than we are sometimes led to believe.

I think we also need to be realistic, and to remind ourselves that, apart from public worship, many of the clergy have themselves effectively given up praying, with dire long-term results on their ministry. This gap often goes back to inadequate training in theological college, where people have not been encouraged to find a pattern of praying that helps them individually, and so have come, wrongly, to the conclusion that somehow they are 'not good at it'. This naturally leads to a sense of considerable guilt, which in turn makes them reluctant to talk with anyone about it. But the joy encountered in clergy who, perhaps quite late on in their ministry, at last find a meaningful way of praying makes the task of direction a rewarding privilege. How much better if everyone in training went as a matter of course to talk with someone on a regular basis about their prayer life.

Another area of need for direction lies in the limitations of some pastoral counselling, which in starting from secular models of counselling has made it difficult for people to use 'God-talk'. Written from an evangelical standpoint, Roger Hurding's *Roots and Shoots*[1] provides an invaluable and comprehensive guide to the various styles of pastoral counselling in relation to the welter of secular styles. We shall be discussing the difference between direction and counselling later on, but it is important to start from a recognition that many are coming to look for a director today *because* so much pastoral counselling is inadequately grounded in the reality and omnipresence of God.

It is in this omnipresence of God that the real task of direction lies: the Inner City report, liberation theology, the place of industry and commerce – all the work in these areas must begin (must it not?) with each individual's awareness of God at work all around them at all times. 'Where has God been at work in your life in the last twenty-four hours?', is perhaps the most basic of all questions to do with spiritual direction, because it is to do with awareness and blindness, with openness and shut-upness. In an early session on one of our spiritual direction courses I invited members to go off in pairs for forty minutes and share the areas in which they could perceive that God had been at work in their lives in the past week, and heard one pair going away complaining that I had set aside far too much time for the exercise – they would cover it in ten minutes. Yet here, surely, lies something at the very heart of being a Christian; and to help individuals, however hesitant they are as Christians, towards a greater awareness of where God has been at work in their world must be one of the most valuable tasks of ministry.

If we can see direction in some such way as this: 'Where has God been at work in my life in the past twenty-four hours?', then we remove direction from the hothouse into an area of relevance for everybody. Then *with* that growing awareness of God at work, people's Christian faith begins to come to life – and with it their *prayer life* also begins to come alive.

This approach to direction also makes it clear that the *whole* of life is within the scope of direction. Nothing is irrelevant to direction. Thomas Merton quotes the Russian story of the director who was reproved by his colleagues for spending too much time talking with an old woman about the care of her turkeys. 'But her *whole life* is in those turkeys,' replied the director.

There *are* limits to direction, but in assessing the need of individuals or groups for direction, an important factor lies in helping people to relate their everyday world of work and family and friendships and play to God's will for them, and so to include the bad as well as the good in their prayer. This being so, we can never say that any Christian is not sufficiently mature or aware for direction of some simple kind, for it lies at the heart of what we are about to be open to the pressure of God upon us, and to perceive that pressure either at the time or retrospectively.

Christianity is essentially about relationships: about God's relationship with us and about the quality of our relationship with each other. Not all Christians, sadly, can be noted for the quality of their relationships, as becomes apparent at almost any Parochial Church Council or other church committee meeting. Through the ongoing, developing relationship of spiritual direction, I believe that Christians can come not only to a deeper relationship with God, but by the quality of that direction relationship to a fuller, more healthy relationship with other people. It is not necessarily advisable that we share the whole of ourselves with other people, but in general the more of ourselves we open to others, the more others will feel able to share of themselves with us, and the deeper, warmer and more genuine our relationships will become.

It follows that a director who has a withdrawn or cold personality will be of only limited help to others. Christianity is about being human, and directors, far from being aloof from humanity, need to have an openness and warmth, an ability to share themselves and so encourage others to share *themselves* in a maturing relationship which, God willing, may come to have just a little of the quality of God's relationship with us all. The direction relationship should be one of a whole person meeting another whole person: the antithesis of certain therapeutic and counselling models where the therapist or counsellor is a sort of reflecting board for projections of various kinds, and not a real whole person. (To me, the latter sort of 'meeting' has little in common with real relationships, either with God or with others. There may be a place for it in certain approaches to therapy, but not in direction, which is about two people encountering each other in their wholeness in the presence of their Creator.)

How far the business of being a Christian in the world can best be considered in groups rather than individually is certainly a matter for discussion. However, my experience suggests that a one-to-one basis is best when considering individual prayer patterns, and that in practice far less time is needed to help people to talk at depth about their families and work in a one-to-one relationship, than in a group. Probably both can be useful. But so much emphasis has been placed on group work in recent years that I believe the time has come to assess, firstly, whether one-to-one work does not enable people to share quite early on in the Christian journey matters they would never share in a group, and secondly, whether one-to-one work, *because* of this greater openness, really requires so much extra expenditure of time.

Because direction, unlike counselling or therapy with its interminable sessions, does not normally require frequent meetings, a director can 'hold' many more people than can a therapist.

Most important of all, as suggested in the first chapter, direction is not essentially problem-centred but growth-centred – concerned with the development of those already basically healthy in Christ, rather than with sorting out difficulties and dis-ease. All too little attention tends to be paid to the fact that Christians *grow*, and need changing patterns of spirituality as a *result* of that growth.

We shall look in the last chapter at how parish strategy might be adapted to make direction a fairly central factor of parish life, but already there is an acute need for more competent directors to fulfil the clamant demands, quite apart from the *latent* needs and possibilities on every side.

3   Patterns of Direction

The late Martin Thornton in his book *Spiritual Direction*,[1] argues that 'holiness' is a less important factor in helpful direction than knowledge. He says, very reasonably, that because someone is perceived to be a 'holy' person and has found a way of prayer which has helped to bring him or her close to God, that is not a sufficient qualification for becoming a good director, because there may be a wish to impose that pattern of prayer upon everyone else. That holy person may well know only one way to God. This is, sadly, a not infrequent phenomenon, and one exacerbated by the spate of 'how to' books, which seem to suggest that the way to God is a matter of works rather than of grace, and that somehow if we have the right technique and the right teacher we shall reach some great moment of enlightenment. The danger is further fostered by the current interest in eastern methods of meditation, which even more acutely give the impression that the task is entirely up to us, and not to God, whether we develop along the path of prayer.

Thornton rightly dwells at length on the need for anyone who aspires to help others in their spiritual path to be aware of the *variety* of ways to God, and to find what is the most helpful path for each directee. But, as already suggested, the needs are too great for direction to be confined to the tiny trickle of people who would meet Thornton's stringent requirements of knowledge and training.

I am reminded of my early days of training in marital counselling, when budding counsellors agonized at length over what they might do in some hypothetical case of unimaginable complexity; and of training lay parish visitors, who immediately fear the first questions asked of them will be something to do with the doctrine of the Trinity or Anselm's interpretation of the Atonement.

As anyone who has done a reasonable amount of direction will know, the greater part of our time is spent on quite simple and basic worries and questions that do not require Thornton's 'assault course' training, which sometimes seems to assume that the director is expected to produce 'answers'. If the director believes that the Holy Spirit is the real director, then there will be an openness to the situation which will not attempt to force a

15

particular way upon the directee. The director is less a person who supplies answers than one who suggests questions for the directee to think and pray about. What I believe is called for is a greater trust in the indwelling Holy Spirit within each person, and a belief that each person, in discussion with another, is likely to uncover what is their own right path. Good direction is to do with trusting that the Holy Spirit is at work in each directee, and allowing them freedom to discuss their own path, not necessarily during the direction session but in the thinking and praying they do afterwards. As in counselling, the real work is frequently done by the client *after* the session.

So while I believe Thornton is right to warn us that the director must not force his own way on the client, and that technical knowledge is a good thing, I should want to have as my keywords, even more than knowledge, *holiness*, *sensitivity*, *insight* and *trust* in the Holy Spirit's guiding into all truth.

I am also a little cautious, on reading Thornton, lest the emphasis in direction becomes too 'head' oriented. This can be difficult for a director who is an intellectual, not greatly in touch with his or her own feelings. But the majority of people we shall be encountering will work rather more according to the dynamic of the feelings and the heart than to the logic of the head. One is not necessarily better than the other, but sensitivity to others is to do with awareness of feelings, with being in touch with our own feelings as well as with those of the directee, and as we shall see, awareness is a basic director's skill. It is a skill with which some people are endowed quite naturally, and my guess is that most people who find themselves being used as directors without having sought it or without any particular training, are both sensitive to others, and in touch with their own feelings. We shall develop this point in the next chapter, but I refer to it now because the difference between 'head' and 'heart' delineates different styles of direction, and may well account for why some may find even a well-known director who works mainly at 'head' level while they work mainly at 'heart' level not very helpful. Concern for technique and knowledge must never get in the way of concern for relationship or lead to our giving insufficient attention to the interaction between client and director and the relationship between both and God. Every person is a *new* person, but Thornton leaves me with the impression more of a doctor presenting the right kind of pill for a patient's disease than of someone assisting in a developing relationship which will always be new, fresh, unexpected and different from any other relationship It *may* help me to know how de Caussade or Ignatius prayed, but neither I nor my client are de Caussade or Ignatius, and our relationship with God will be unique.

This part of the discussion is at root to do with the extent to which the director is directive or non-directive. Most of the points at issue in the world of therapy and counselling also raise their heads in the world of direction. There are times when a director may feel it right to be literally 'directive', sensing that something is seriously wrong, or that quite strong reinforcement would be helpful. But on the whole the director's task lies more in the non-directive area of helping directees to a greater awareness of the reality of God and of how God is at work in their lives in ways they have not yet perceived, so that in that greater awareness they may find the path God is opening up for them, and their relationship with God in prayer may be deepened. This approach avoids the dangers of dependence upon the director, and allows the client to grow and mature in a true reliance upon God. In other words, directors are to be used as signposts rather than props.

There are also differences between what I would call our English approach to direction and the general impression given by the flood of books now arriving from the United States. The Americans seem to be going in for what some of us here might consider a hothouse type of direction. Their expectation may well be of initial weekly (or even more frequent) direction, eventually settling down to a monthly meeting. My guess is that people in the States are accustomed to being in therapy or counselling, and that to meet with a director only, say, quarterly, might for them seem minimal. If the situation allows for such concentration, well and good, but there is, I believe, a danger not only of undue dependence upon the director, but equally that direction may drift all too easily into counselling or problem-solving, or may become trivialized and 'precious'. Further, the realities of parish life and, in England at least, the cost of such concentrated ministry, would suggest far less frequent meeting. If direction is in some limited sense to be available for all Christians, then the director's time needs to be spread more widely.

However, when working with people for the first time it may

indeed be helpful to begin with more frequent sessions, particularly for those who appear to have compartmentalized their life and can see little or no activity of God or relevance of Christianity in their place of work, or to be carrying an inordinate amount of unnecessary guilt that springs from a misinterpretation of the gospel and cannot be eased away by anything as distant as a quarterly meeting. The home-based retreats outlined in Chapter 7 have proved their worth in getting new people started in being directed with an intensive half-hour a day for five days. But I would be cautious about expecting to meet as often as monthly in a normal direction relationship, which might continue in some instances for many years. The demands are too great and there is the ever-present danger of dependency and infantilism.

As we consider different patterns of direction, let us look now at the *boundaries* of direction, an important question which is almost inextricably tied up with the distinction between direction and counselling, and with the even more difficult distinction between direction and pastoral care.

For some, spiritual direction is a clear-cut task of helping a person in their prayer-life, concerned with work and family and relationships only in so far as they affect that person's rule of life, which has been formulated primarily to assist in the development of that prayer life. I should be the last to denigrate this approach; it has the advantage of clarity – we certainly know where we are up to. More importantly, it puts first things first: we have come to talk about God and it is God we shall talk about.

If we extend the horizons of direction, however, we shall need to be much more circumspect and wary, lest God becomes pushed to the periphery. Barry and Connolly[2] are insistent that the director should be constantly alert to sessions where the presence and activity of God seem to have little to do with the discussion. They counsel probing whether there is being what they call 'resistance' to God in these aspects of the client's life. The Jesuit tradition as a whole is very helpful in bringing us back again and again to the present reality and experience of God.

But if God is concerned with the whole of life, then the whole of life is to be directed by God; and just as the turkeys in Thomas Merton's story were a proper topic for spiritual direction, so relationships, moral problems at work, and wider political and other issues will be valid areas of discussion in a direction session. We cannot separate the 'spiritual' from the secular: there is only one world and all of it belongs to God.

I find it increasingly difficult to be dogmatic about all this. To some extent the boundaries we place on our direction sessions will depend upon our own skills and training. In an ideal world I believe that all spiritual directors would have at least a basic competence in counselling, though obviously not all counsellors would be directors. I detect in many directors of an older generation a paternalism which inhibits growth (in themselves as well as their clients), and which all too often maintains an authoritarian pattern that distinguishes clergy from laity as leaders and led in a way no longer acceptable (if indeed it ever was so). Direction, in the sense in which I am using the word, with the real director as the Holy Spirit, is a ministry of trust and letting go. A basic knowledge of counselling will often be the quickest and easiest way of growing out of authoritarian patterns of direction. I think it also needs to be stressed that while books are helpful, neither counselling nor direction can really be learned except by doing and experiencing – and by being counselled and being directed oneself.

If the director is also by training a counsellor, he or she may sometimes change from a 'direction' mode to a 'counsellor' mode. Where there is a purely psychological problem getting in the way of spiritual growth, it will be worth while stopping to look at it. The important thing is for the director to be aware that the session is no longer looking immediately at the God-relationship, and to ensure that the sessions do not get permanently 'stuck' in a counselling mode. I quite often suggest to directees that we have come up against something that may need a bit of extra work done on it, and that we might change from, say, a quarterly meeting to monthly or weekly until we have sorted out this problem, and then revert to our longer time-scale. This helps to make some kind of a distinction between discussion which is primarily based upon God and discussion which for the time being concentrates on human relationships. But the distinction is not always so clear-cut, and a director without counselling training may need to choose between looking at the problem as well as he or she can, or suggesting a suitable counsellor to whom the client might turn. Referral needs a great deal of caution – it is easy to try to refer when it might be better to stay alongside because a relationship has been built up with one particular person who may have more skill and insight than they realize. One eminent Christian psychotherapist has said that often it is better to send someone to a warm, caring Christian pastor with no technical skills than to a technically clever non-religious counsellor who may be lacking in love.

Where problems in relationships or other psychological problems occur in direction, the best initial course rather than referral, is usually for the director to discuss the client anonymously, with due regard to confidentiality, with a trained and caring counsellor or therapist, who will listen and perhaps assist the director to stay with the client, and will make suggestions on the handling of the problem. Again and again, it seems to me, if our faith is about relationships, then direction and the whole Christian enterprise is about relationships. This needs a measure of trust that the Holy Spirit can often work through undemanding and self-giving love, and not always necessarily through secular techniques.

If direction can on the one hand shade off into counselling, on other occasions direction may shade outwards into work-supervision. This is particularly true where clergy are directing other clergy. The client then knows that the director is familiar with the kind of work he is doing; he knows that in a relationship of trust and friendship he can talk about his failures – and God knows how reluctant clergy are to talk about their failures in the usual clergy gatherings or with the church hierarchy. Indeed for many clergy, clergy gatherings are frequently destructive of confidence because all around seem to be proudly parading their 'successes', making the sensitive priest feel even more incompetent. For years now I have deliberately tried at clergy gatherings to talk about my failures because it seems to cheer other people up considerably, and helps them to discuss their own. I believe there is important work to be done on the neurotic need many clergy have to advertise their successes and deny their failures.

A clerical directee, then, in the confidence and friendship of a direction session will often bring work problems into the open. It is easy to say that these should be discussed in another setting – in a work support group, maybe – but such may be a counsel of perfection, and, after all, the pastor's work is intimately tied up with his or her relationship with God. God's activity in such a person's life will almost certainly be at its most immediate in the context of parish work.

This is equally true of so-called secular work: once people are able to understand and perceive something of the influence of God in their everyday activity, that will become an important area for discussion. The morality of decisions they may have to make, the area of relationships and staff appointments and conflicts – for the Christian all these are vital areas of God's activity, and the director can expect to help the client to trace back many such dilemmas to basic Christian doctrines of Creation, of Stewardship, of Work and so on. The important proviso is that all this takes place within an awareness of God, and is not a discussion in purely secular terms – also, that it forms only one part of the discussion, and that discussion about work is not an escape from or resistance to discussion about the more direct relationship with God in prayer and worship. Clergy – even some who come for direction – can be past masters at avoiding the real issue and concealing the barrenness of their prayer life.

So what, then, is the relationship between direction and counselling, and between direction and pastoral care?

As indicated above, I find it increasingly hard to be dogmatic. In many areas of Christian life we may have a variety of different starting points and yet end up at the same destination. For example, when Christian Stewardship was more in vogue than it is today, how did we define stewardship? Did we think of it simply in terms of the form sent out inviting people to think about their time, money and talents? Or was Christian Stewardship something to do with how you worked out the whole of your life in relationship to God, including your approach to ecology and conservation, your choice of vocation or career as well as how you worked out your prayer and study and worship? Stewardship could effectively be a starting point for consideration of the whole Christian vocation.

In much the same way it is possible on the one hand to start from spiritual direction in the closely defined way in which we began this chapter, or on the other hand to see it as encompassing the whole of the Christian life, and different directors will draw the line at different points, according to their skills and abilities. Much the same can be said of pastoral care. Without undue cynicism one could define the view some people have of pastoral care as not much more than the vicar going round to have tea with old people and talk about their illnesses. Or one can use the term 'pastoral care', as does Howard Clinebell,[3] for example, to encompass a concern for the whole of individual and community life under God, including spiritual growth. Thus we end up at much the same point having set out from the several different starting points of Christian Stewardship, Pastoral Care and Spiritual Direction.

This comprehensive view of pastoral care and counselling held by people like Clinebell makes it hard to draw entirely clear-cut lines between that world and the world of spiritual direction. Ken Leech, in his fine discussion of the point in *Soul Friend*, envisages a far less Christian-oriented kind of counselling than is often nowadays the case, taking as his model for discussion systems of counselling based squarely on secular patterns. Much counselling is a response to a problem: most of us seek counselling only when we perceive ourselves to have a problem, but Clinebell's growth-centred approach to pastoral care sets his counselling in a wider perspective. Nevertheless it remains true that most counselling is problem-centred, relatively short-term, mainly psycho-dynamically oriented and generally intensive. Spiritual direction is growth-centred, may continue for many years, is mainly theologically oriented and takes place usually at more widely spaced intervals.

Furthermore, the spiritual director will always have as his *primary* concern the path in prayer and life which the Holy Spirit holds out to the client; psychological concerns are secondary to the main task. In counselling, the task may frequently end before issues of God have come seriously into the picture: in direction God is the starting point. Roger Hurding,[4] in his comprehensive survey of styles of counselling and psychotherapy quotes David Porter thus: 'at no time is counselling an attempt to convert or to unduly influence a client to any particular creed or philosophy of life'. This is a view which would be challenged by many types of evangelical counselling, but the influence of Carl Rogers and his followers remains dominant in both secular and Christian counselling, where the emphasis is on non-directiveness. The spiritual director, however, while usually equally non-directive, works within an assumption of Christian belief. Indeed, without some readiness to go along with such an assumption a person is unlikely to come to a director at all.

We are therefore working, in general, within a shared framework of belief about life – though the misconceptions of Christian belief and practice among quite committed Christians can often be disturbing, especially on the point of guilt.

One of the most important points in Leech's discussion of counselling and direction is that all too often counselling has as its stated or implied aim *adjustment* to society as it is. People come to the counsellor with problems about their relationships to individuals or to the world in which they are living, and the counsellor accepts the task of enabling them to adjust to that world. Leech quotes one therapist, Kathleen Heasman, who defines counselling as 'a relationship in which one person endeavours to help another to understand and solve his difficulties of adjustment to society'.

But the director would see most of society itself as a far greater 'problem' than most of the problems of a client. In Christian terms it would be entirely wrong to *be* fully adjusted to the kind of society in which we live, with all its injustices and selfishness and greed. Christians may well have to go on living in anguish for the awfulness of much of man's world; and for many that anguish will provide the impetus driving them to work for change and improvement. So in direction the task is not to find the most comfortable way to live in society, but to try to discern how the Holy Spirit may be guiding us to play our part in establishing something of the Kingdom of God in our part of the world. Spiritual direction has social and political overtones. The fact that it usually takes place in a one-to-one situation does not mean that it is confined to cultivating hothouse 'gardens of the soul', any more than prayer undertaken alone is necessarily a selfish enterprise.

We now turn to the much debated question of the relationship between direction and sacramental confession, because this also influences styles of direction. One of the purposes of this book is to encourage not only clergy, but lay women and men to become more closely involved in spiritual direction. Not all clergy have the necessary sensitivity and insight, so if a parish or congregation is to provide this important function it will need to be undertaken by lay people.

Where the director is a priest, the client has the option of using the same priest as a confessor or of making a formal confession elsewhere. My experience over the years suggests, however, that where a close relationship develops with the director, this is the best place for the pronouncement of absolution. After talking things through in depth with one person, formal confession to another will be experienced as just that: formal – and rather empty. My practice with my own director is to use each visit to him in whatever way seems best – sometimes a formal confession is a part of the visit, sometimes the discussion carried out informally has the nature of confession and it seems right, however informal it has been, to have absolution pronounced at the end. On other occasions we simply talk and part. I adopt a similar practice with those who come to me, encouraging them to use the time as seems best to them. This may seem very lax and haphazard, and a lot depends upon the tradition with which people are familiar. But I do know that, for many, old-fashioned formal confession becomes very empty after the experience of a deeper relationship, and if the whole direction session is seen as being under God, seeking *His* direction, then the informal confession does seem to me to be being made to God. I come back to the quality of relationships – in old-fashioned formal confession there seems a less adequate concept of a deep relationship, either with God or with the confessor, than there is within a more intensive one-to-one session.

Where the director is not a priest it seems to me that, again, practice should vary with what is most helpful for the individual directee. If there has been a tradition of formal confession, that may well continue with the person's normal confessor, though in such instances it is well for penitents to make clear to confessors that they are under direction elsewhere. There are other instances too, where even if sacramental confession has not been a part of a person's past, it may well be important (particularly at the beginning of the direction, when all sorts of untidy elements may come tumbling out of the past), for the client to make a sacramental confession and experience the release and joy of absolution and acceptance.

In all this, temperament and personality are naturally important – the plain fact is that sacramental acts are more meaningful and important to some than to others, and the sooner a potential director recognizes these important differences the better. For many, the simple release of anxiety and guilt and unacceptability to another trusted person will provide the necessary realization of the love of God. The talking will itself be the sacrament. I am sure that in many instances it would be wrong to talk of formal confession; the lay director can pray with the directee, or read one or two suitable Scripture sentences to do with forgiveness, and then sit quietly together for a time. Thanksgiving for the forgiveness of God can be offered alone at home later on, and the next attendance at the Eucharist can be made the occasion of sealing the awareness of renewal and forgiveness.

I cannot end this chapter on patterns of direction without a word for some who may already feel daunted by the task of direction, and perhaps believe that no-one is ever likely to come to them and ask them outright to 'take them on'. I should hate to make the role of spiritual director seem so exalted that caring, praying and sensitive people might feel it could never be for them. And this is where I come back to my earlier point: that it is often very hard to make a clear-cut distinction between spiritual direction and good pastoral care.

Time and time again what happens is that, in discussion with others, some of us find ourselves being asked, out of the blue, questions about prayer, about belief, about decisions. We begin to feel that somehow, for reasons only known to those who ask, we must give the impression of having grasped something of the love of God. Often the questions asked are only the tip of the iceberg: given the opportunity there will be others. The questioners may never have talked with anyone in any depth about what they believe or think they believe. They may be burdened with great areas of unnecessary guilt, misperceptions of what the Christian gospel is about, worries about relationships, concern about prayer being dead, not wanting to pray or not knowing how to pray. This is not the occasion for attempting to 'solve' a 'problem' with an instant answer. You probably do not have an answer, and to try to respond on the spot may be helping less than you have it in you to help. Here is the occasion to ask the questioner, 'Would you like to come round and talk it through over coffee this evening?' – or whenever. Real Christian growth needs time and space. Don't be put off by the occasions when you get a polite refusal: that is bound to happen.

Try to respond to the person concerned *as a person*. Don't think out how you are going to 'answer' their question; simply talking it through may enable them to find their own answer. Stay with *their* experiences and feelings, rather than quoting Bible texts at them or using theological language which may mean something to you (does it?!) but will probably mean little to them. Try to remember that the unseen 'Other' in the meeting is Christ – the Christ who is in every human person, who is in you, who is in the space between you – and look for all the good, positive potential in them, so that their understanding of love can develop, so that their power *to* love can develop. You are concerned about their growing relationship with God, yes, but God is in the present, and for the moment your concern has to be his presence within your relationship with them.

If our discussion with others takes place in this frame of mind, whether we begin with formal prayer or with a silence the whole session will itself be a kind of prayer in which we shall be attentive both to the other person and to our own feelings and reactions. We shall be asking ourselves, even if it is not yet appropriate to ask it of the other person, 'Where is God in all this?' But we shall not be dogmatic in our statements; rather we may make suggestions – 'I wonder whether . . . ? Do you think . . . ? Does it feel as if . . . ? Might it be helpful to . . . ? Had you thought of . . . ?'

If we avoid giving instruction and directions or imagined answers to problems it will help us to avoid forming a relationship of undue dependency. Dependency is not always wrong – maturity is indeed about *inter*-dependency and for Christians to recognize their dependence not only upon God but upon others is a part of being grown up. Undue dependency comes when one adult relates to another consistently as a child to a parent, and fails to look critically at that other, or when there is a degree of emotional involvement beyond what should reasonably be expected from the limited relationship of discussion and direction.

In some such way as this many people of sensitivity and prayerfulness have discovered a ministry of inestimable help and value to others, and a ministry in which the fledgeling director will also grow from the confidence shown by others: 'I never realized I'd got it in me!' is a fairly typical and very humble response, because all gifts are of God and all that is good in direction is the work of God. The director is simply a person who tries to be sufficiently open to be used by God in helping others.

4   The First Session

In attempting to understand the initial process of direction we shall assume, not that as a neophyte director we have tentatively invited someone to come and talk on a one-off basis, but that someone has come to see us with a view to our 'taking them on' for direction on a more or less long term basis.

If we are new to the task, we shall be feeling unsure of ourselves. What on earth have we let ourselves in for? Just what are we trying to do? What shall we say? Have we any right to attempt to direct, or any resources whatever to justify our presumption? Our visitor, we feel, is going to expect us to be expert on all sorts of things we feel we know little about.

But the likelihood is that our own anxiety is as nothing compared to that of the person coming to see us! Our potential directee, if the work is to be of any deep value, knows that he or she will need to be talking about intensely personal matters, about weakness and failure and guilt, and in nine cases out of ten admitting to an inadequate prayer life or perhaps a prayer life which has broken down completely. And on top of this an experienced director, unfamiliar except by reputation, may well be seen as an authoritative, even condemning figure.

Martin Thornton is rightly scornful of direction which drifts into mere cosy chat, but nevertheless it is very important not to hurry too much in the first session. A little time of general chat will help both sides to lose some of the wrong projections, to begin by meeting simply as two human individuals and start building up a relationship. This is the point where my earlier emphasis on the director being a whole person has its value – most counsellors will fail to give any information about themselves, and fend off any personal questions. In the direction friendship, which will probably be developing in home surroundings and not in the counselling room, the director can begin to emerge as a real person.

The setting may well be the home, but it is important that there should be no interruptions. This is easier said than done in most houses, especially vicarages, but a real attempt needs to be made to frustrate interruptions, because a deep train of discussion can be lost for ever in the face of a telephone call or doorbell. I believe we should also always make clear that a whole hour has been set aside for the discussion. Beyond an hour, there is likely to be either repetition or a lack of real concentration on one side or on both, and a clear indication of how much time is available helps the client to bring out difficult matters. Every counsellor is familiar with the difficult and most important topic being delayed until the client reaches the doorstep on the way out, so letting the opportunity slip. The same is common in direction, and such last-minute confidences need to be held in the director's memory until the next meeting.

Practice differs on keeping notes. Except in special cases it is certainly embarrassing for a director to be taking notes during a session, but it may help, after the session, to record one or two key points or topics which seem to need further exploration. If we are seeing a lot of people we shall find it impossible to hold the sharpness of key points over what may be a three-month gap before the next session.

Usually a number of practical points need to be sorted out in this first session, for example, frequency of meeting. As suggested above, my own practice, (though like all practices infinitely variable to meet individual need) is to suggest meeting monthly for a while, at the start, and thereafter quarterly. I believe that the most valuable work is done by the client alone in the light of what has gone on in the direction session – or rather, by the client alone with God. The director is only a kind of midwife, and in my view should keep quite a low profile, which is why I am not happy about the transatlantic practice of weekly meetings, tailing off to monthly meetings. We also need to make it quite clear (and this can be done without embarrassment at the start of the session), that if either side feels the relationship is not going to work, then it should be ended without any sense of failure on either side. No director worth the name will be in the least offended, for none of us is competent to direct every type of personality.

Perhaps most difficult in the question of compatibility is the increasing frequency (to be commended) with which ordinands and others in vocational training are recommended to have a director. Such people will sometimes come uncertain as to what direction is all about and unsure whether they even want it, and it is not always easy to differentiate between this uncertainty (and even a measure of resentment) and incompatibility. There is always the temptation for the director to pull a rabbit out of the hat, as it were, to show the potential directee that the system 'works'. This temptation is to be resisted, and the director should try not to feel any pressure to 'perform', but to be even more open and prayerful than usual and to recognize the reality of the person who has come for direction.

As we try to formulate some kind of contract for the relationship we may also want to sort out what (if anything) is to happen about sacramental confession, and, in order that our client will feel at home, to decide whether or not our sessions will begin and/or end with silence or spoken prayer. There is a lot to be said for beginning with silence. Not only does it help a client who may have had a difficult journey to centre down and relax, it makes clear that the session has God as its main focus, and the absence of verbal prayer ensures that the client is not imposed upon by any hidden agenda from the director. Those unfamiliar with counselling may be anxious if silences occur in the course of the hour, but these can be most productive, and may be an indication that the client is trying to be receptive to insights from God.

One further practical point is whether direction can be mutual. The director needs to have a director, or, if we prefer to use a different term, a 'spiritual friend'. Some may find it helpful to 'exchange' direction; but if this is done it should be in clear-cut sessions, so that one partner does not receive more attention and time than the other, less dominant partner. Dorothy Devers, in *Faithful Friendship*,[1] has worked out some helpful exercises for this kind of relationship. It is an idea which can he helpful to two people who are both starting along the path of direction, particularly where there has been a problem in finding an experienced director. And if we are to see direction as being in any sense for every serious Christian, this line perhaps should be given more attention. But I think it should probably be regarded more as spiritual friendship than direction, and somewhere along the line there should be someone outside the twosome occasionally monitoring the process, lest it become too cosy and inward-looking, or be affected by shades of envy, or even turn into what counsellors would call a 'gruesome twosome'. If we are sharing mutual spiritual friendship I think we shall become *aware* that there is a difference between this and direction, and that some measure of outside direction is needed as well, however helpful the spiritual friendship may be.

So, sitting together for the first time, the director is likely to be wondering even more insistently than we have so far suggested, 'Just what am I trying to do?' In the case of clients who have, in some sense, 'been sent', the director may need to spell out what direction has to offer; but remembering that we are concerned primarily with our clients' needs, and with the action of God in their lives, it is probably better to begin by asking them just what *they* want, and what *they* are expecting.

Right from the start the director needs to strike a balance. It is true that what really matters is each client's growing ability to accord their way of life with what they perceive to be God's will, and that what the director thinks is of much less importance. So the question, 'What do you think?' is usually much better turned back upon directees until they become clearer about their own thoughts and feelings, and can come to their own decision. Nevertheless, unless the director has a fairly clear general picture of the person concerned (to be clarified and refined in later meetings), it will not be possible to enter helpfully into their world. So the first session must inevitably involve a gentle discovery of a directee's temperament and of 'where they are'.

On the other hand, the director should refrain from too much questioning in this first session, or the seeds of dependency will be sown: the directee will begin to feel, 'Once I've told everything, I'll be able to be directed authoritatively about what to do and how to pray.' So there should be some provisionality about the first few sessions, as we try to build up a relationship rather than fill in a predetermined questionnaire.

The director will therefore begin to build up a picture of the directee in an indirect way:

What does the client find helpful or unhelpful in ways of praying?

What is their prayer pattern (if any)?

What are the pressures on time which make prayer difficult?

What is the pattern of public worship?

What is found helpful or unhelpful in public worship?

Is it easier to pray alone? in groups with others? in church?

Is reading ('pious' or 'secular') an important part of the pattern or not?

What image (or images) of God do they have? (For some people God may be represented in *feelings* rather than in words or images.)

Do they relate most naturally to God as Father and Creator, or to Jesus, or to the Holy Spirit? (The God ahead of us, the God beside us, the God within us.)

What is their general life situation and how closely is their awareness of God or their realization of the relevance of God integrated with their work, their relationships, their pleasures and relaxation?

How far is God experienced when alone, in church, in relationships, in groups, in the natural world, in art, music, dance, drama, mathematics?

Is their prayer mainly concerned with speaking, or with using their imagination, thinking, being quiet, listening?

What gets censored in prayer? (For example, can they be angry with God? can they take their sexuality to God?)

What is their self-image? Low? High?

How free are they in the expression of warm or negative feelings to others?

What is their faith history?

Having read these questions, I suggest that readers go back to the start and spend quite a lot of time on them, asking them of themselves before even dreaming of asking them of anyone else! These are only a few of many areas of importance in the direction relationship, and in no way would it be appropriate to attempt to raise all of these in a single session.

I quite often try to raise the question 'What do you want?' in a deeper form than merely the setting up of the contract. When Jesus asked a blind man what he wanted, the blind man had an immediate answer: 'I want my sight back.' The directee (and for that matter, the director) is less likely to have such a clear cut answer if the question is posed by imagining that the physical presence of Jesus comes into the room. But unless we know what we *really* want of life – unless we know what we want at our deepest level – we shall be lacking both in self-awareness and in knowing what is our true direction in life. The path we are actually taking may be pulling against a much *deeper* want, which may be either more *un*selfish or more *selfish* than our outwardly apparent direction.

Having established what we really want Jesus to do for us, the next question seems to be equally searching: 'Why that and not something else?' Over the years *what* we want – and why – is likely to change many times, and it is a question worth frequent pondering in ourselves no less than in our directees.

Sometimes at the end of the first session we shall be asked outright for the next appointment, or we shall find that time is needed to think it over. If the directee is happy then I find it best to make the next appointment there and then, but never in any sense to press for a decision. The directee may not be sure that we are the right person for them, and may need time to sort out their reactions. Above all, it is important to leave our visitor without any sense of being pressurized to come back, and without feeling that either they or we have somehow failed if it does not seem right to continue. As time goes on we shall probably find a wider range of people able to cope with us and we with them.

5 The Ongoing Task

'We come to God,' declared St Augustine, 'by love, not by navigation.' That saying should be engraved on the heart of every director: not by techniques, but by grace: the loving relationship of direction, the loving yearning towards God of directee and director alike, and the growing awareness of God's love reaching out towards us or welling up from within the very heart of our being. This, rather than an obsession with technique or 'how to', is what spiritual direction is about.

Director and directee begin from their relationship with God, and both gradually shed the old fallen self and 'put on Christ'. 'Discipleship is a renaming of myself by a process of identifying with the person I am called to follow.' 'Because the disciples fail to grasp the identity of *Jesus*, they cannot understand who they are themselves.'[1] It is in knowing increasingly the reality of Christ that we come to know our true selves – that which we have it in us to become.

It follows that the director will be constantly alert to abilities and talents and insights lying dormant in the directee, just waiting to be freed for use. Talents so often lie unused because of a lack of confidence, and the lack of confidence itself takes its origin in a lack of being valued by others, or in not fully realizing how we are valued and loved by God. The director is to some extent reinforcing in the directee the as yet only dimly perceived love and acceptance of God.

Over the years I have perceived especially in married women who have had to give up a profession or a career in order to bring up their family, a considerable lack of confidence in themselves. Before they can return to either paid or voluntary work outside the family they may need to work through this lack of confidence, and be affirmed in the talents they still have which have been necessarily laid aside for a period. One of the great strengths of spiritual direction in an active Christian community, as against basic counselling within the four walls of a counselling room, is that out in the Christian community there are resources for enabling people to grow in confidence through friendships, and through being asked to take on smaller tasks that will help to build up their confidence until they are able to take on something more commensurate with their innate abilities.

As our identity gradually changes into our *true* identity in Christ, so not only our pattern of living, but our pattern of *prayer* changes. The typical prayer of the young child is a prayer of simple joy and wonder and thanks, with uninhibited asking at the heart of it. The typical prayer of the adolescent is a somewhat bewildered one in a world which is now perceived, perhaps with some fear, as a much bigger world than was once imagined. For adolescents the size of the world, both their outer and also their inner world, makes it necessary for them to relate more powerfully and emotively to others for support and identity – a relating further bonded by the bewildering growth of sexual awareness and of their ability as near-adults to hurt other people. The adolescent is continually discovering the world to be ever larger and more bewildering, and extreme swings of emotion are therefore to be expected in their relationship with God, no less than in their relationships with other people.

The responses of childhood and adolescence, though they change with later phases of life, are not to be totally lost. Throughout our lives we need to hold on to the child within us and, as appropriate, express that child in play and wonder and a sense of fun. Equally in our relationship to God we need to hold on to something of the wonder and delight of the child, with the child's simple thanking and asking, the child's spontaneity, the child's sense of wonder. In the same way, the adult will also benefit from retaining something of the adolescent's awe and bewilderment as he ponders the unimaginable greatness of God.

Nevertheless, we need to continue to grow. Ways of relating to other people which are attractive in a child become annoying if continued into adolescence, while the understandable self-centredness of the puzzled adolescent is inappropriate to the demands of adulthood. In the same way the director will be awake to inappropriate and immature ways of relating to God. All too many adults have a child's quasi-magical belief in God as someone who will wave a magic wand and make everything better. Countless times one has to work with adults, even middle-aged or elderly people, who in bereavement or other difficulty have not matured out of a concept of a God who will somehow 'kiss and make it better'. The Cross has not yet become a part of their understanding of God. Often this 'magic' view of religion runs quite deep: people have an acute sense of being let down if tragedy strikes, and revert to an angry infantile stance or give up belief in God altogether. A director may encounter this in apparently quite mature Christians who have in later life been stressed beyond any point they had previously experienced, and who have been 'good' Christians in not letting out their anger and resentment in earlier years. It all comes together later on in an explosion of bewildering, frightening anger and incomprehension that God should 'allow' all this to happen.

Young adulthood is a time of outgoingness: careers have to be established, family life cemented. And despite our relaxation of stereotyped male and female roles it is also a time when many men find that in the demands of work they are losing touch with some of the gentler, more feminine aspects of themselves; while women, still very much tied to child-rearing, may find themselves getting out of touch with their more outgoing, masculine attributes.

In all this busy-ness, prayer is likely to be fairly sketchy, and the director (particularly if not married) needs to be sensitive to the incessant demands young children make on a mother. Prayer may be brief, intercessory, or confined to short aspirations, or trying to make work into a kind of prayer by doing it as well as possible. Simple awareness of the world around is another helpful way towards prayer in the busy time of life.

In middle age and later, with career established and family grown up, comes the possibility of exploring our lost 'shadow' the masculine and feminine aspects of ourselves; while in prayer life not only can a firm pattern of prayer become established, but directees can as appropriate begin to explore the 'shadow' sides of their prayer life as well. Contemplatives can learn to use their imagination, and imaginative people can learn something of the simplicity of contemplation; thinking people can learn to explore their feelings in prayer and feeling people can learn to use their minds a little. It is a time for quite exciting exploration in prayer if directees are willing to give some time and effort to working on the parts of themselves with which they feel less at home. The objective, of course, is wholeness and freedom.

With the eventide years comes the time to begin to let go – not to cease to enjoy happy memories, but to let go of clutching on to them or being dependent upon them, and even more to stop fretting over all the things we have not achieved and now never will. To cling on to these will only make us resentful and bitter, and tie us to the past when we could be turning to our future in God. As we begin to see our final landfall coming up on the horizon, we may need helping to live each day of the journey more fully in the present, making the most of what we have been given. Just as the last day of a holiday, or the last meal with a loved friend, is the most poignant and powerful, so can the evening years be intensely powerful and beautiful. Spiritually we shall be ready to go when called, and our prayer will reflect that readiness.

So a question we ask members of our spiritual direction courses – 'What time of day on a 24-hour clock is it in your life?' – is worth asking again from time to time. The answer may have more to do with the directee's state of mind than with their age – one not-very-old person responded to that question by saying that for them it was nearly midnight, indicating a fairly profound degree of depression requiring a longish spell of counselling.

For a sustained and wise discussion of the psychiatric dimensions of spiritual direction, the reader would do well to refer to Gerald May's books.[2] At a fairly basic level, it may be worth raising the subject of depression, which features largely in the prayer life as in the emotional life of very many people.

Depression is part of life for the vast majority of us. So it is important for a director to be aware of depression in others, and not leap to the conclusion that a directee is working through some profound 'dark night' when really dealing with a straightforward emotional condition. The imagined glamour of St John of the Cross has not always been a healthy influence on Western spirituality, and people refer glibly to 'dark nights of the soul' with very little idea of what St John was really talking about. It may also be worth reminding ourselves that Eastern spirituality does not live with any automatic expectation of 'dark nights'.

Frequently the director will be dealing with something very ordinary and very simple – overwork, tiredness, stress in family or work relationships, a moral dilemma or moral guilt, anxiety or failure. A director who has no basic counselling knowledge (and sometimes one who has) may well find it best to use the simple technique of distraction so often effective with children, staying lightly on the surface while suggesting rest and relaxation. If we do not have the technical competence, to try to accompany a person into their depression may well either take them down even deeper, whence we are unable to bring them out again, or may (since depression is infectious) drive the director too into depression, which does not help anybody. Only proper training or long experience can guide us as to when it is helpful to go along with someone into their depression, and when it is better to help sufferers to get out of themselves a little.

If a directee's darkness takes the form of being 'unable to pray', we may find it helpful to offer them the 'freedom' of simply not praying for a time and not feeling guilty about it. All too often earlier Christian formation will have induced areas of totally unnecessary guilt, which lead people to imagine great thunderbolts about to descend from heaven if they do not 'keep the rules' and pray faithfully every day. As a result, prayer can become a harassed, depressed and guilt-ridden activity instead of a relaxation, release and point of growth. If the directee can be freed from a neurotic compulsion to pray that arouses guilt whenever prayer-time is missed or concentration less than total – if a period without prayer can be lived through without guilt and without any apparent punishment from the Almighty – then a totally different dynamic of prayer is likely to arise. I begin to pray not because I feel guilty if I *don't* pray; I pray because I feel it would be a worthwhile activity: hard work, like any worthwhile enterprise, but nevertheless something I *want* to do and to explore. God is worth my effort, he is not a Blakeian Nobodaddy waiting to pounce on me if I fail to pray, and even (may it be added) waiting to pounce on me the moment I start being happy or enjoying myself. A fearful number of Christian souls go around the world expecting to have to pay some terrible price for any time they are feeling really happy – a pathetic attitude which squares ill with the Lord who came that we might have Life, and have it in all its fullness!

Directors will rapidly become sensitive to those punishing super-egos which manifest themselves in repeated statements of 'I should' or 'I ought' or 'I have to' or 'I must'. The total replacement of these words in Rational-Emotive Therapy[3] by such phrases as 'I would better' may sound forced and quirky, but it does help us to focus on the sort of super-egos which induce guilt and depression. Where 'ought' plays a large part in the directee's language, some exploration of their concept of God will almost certainly prove helpful.

Depression, as hardly needs to be said, is often the fruit of repressed anger. As I write these words, however, I think of the countless hours I have spent with good Christian people who honestly believe – even in the 1980s – that somehow it is wrong for Christians to be angry.

But anger has to go somewhere. Jesus was angry: Job was angry: the Psalms are *very* angry! 'Let not anger lead you into sin' – yes; 'Let not the sun go down on your anger' – yes. But that is not the same as telling us to 'bottle up' our anger. Suppressing our anger may conceal from another person that we are justifiably feeling hurt, when they *need* to know that they have hurt us, as a necessary correction to their behaviour; when they need to *know* that they are making us angry and hurting us. Frequently, however, anger is suppressed because of a lack of confidence. Some people do not express anger because they fear its consequences – 'They won't go on loving me if I'm angry', or 'They will take reprisals'. Most often people suppress their anger because they know they will not be able to cope with the uncomfortable feelings it will arouse in them, either from their own ill temper or from the angry response of others.

This may seem to border on counselling, but anger so often characterizes under-developed and negative and feeble and depressed Christians that it needs to be raised here. Anger if suppressed repeatedly will result either in depression or in a massive explosion of pent-up resentment totally inappropriate to whatever small stimulus triggers it.

Most harmful of all is the inability to express our anger towards God. There is, I believe, a perfectly valid prayer of anger. I well recall a friend who many years ago was going through a very bad period and told me with disarming honesty, on his way to chapel, that he was off to have his daily battle with God. It was a long battle which resulted initially in a period of atheism and his not being ordained. But because it was properly worked out, it ended in his return to a much more mature faith and a way of expressing that faith in a career which entirely matched his very considerable talents.

That 'battle with God' is important for all of us: God can *take* the anger and use it to help us at times when it is genuinely inappropriate to express it to others.

I recall too a prison chaplain telling me about a prisoner who was serving time for a number of ferocious bodily assaults. Even in prison he had extra time added to his sentence because of his continuing assaults on other prisoners. The chaplain gave the man a wooden crucifix and suggested he should keep it in his pocket, and if he felt tempted to assault another prisoner grip the crucifix and try to transfer the anger to it instead. Some time later the prisoner came to the chaplain and showed him the crucifix crushed into tiny pieces. He had followed the suggestion and by smashing the crucifix had managed to restrain himself from assaulting anyone.

I find it hard to think of a better parable to show where, in the final resort, we need to take our anger for defusing it.

'Darkness', as against anger, may call for other perceptions on the part of the director. Children have their own understanding of God appropriate to their age and development. If, however, as they go through adolescence, they are unable to grow in their understanding of God so as to reach an awareness of him appropriate to their greater awareness of the size of the world, they will – quite rightly, in my view – reject the idea of God. Their understanding of God has to grow with their understanding of this world. In other words, their childish image of God has to some extent to be destroyed if they are to come to a more appropriate understanding of him.

This process of growing in awareness of the size and wonder of the universe is meant to continue throughout our lives, and as we grow in awareness of God's world, so we shall realize that the image of God which we have is inadequate; 'Your God is too small,' as J. B. Phillips expressed it many years ago.

This recognition that our God is too small is one of the major causes of our sense of darkness and of God's absence. Painful though this may be, and long as it may last, it is nevertheless to do with *growth*. We shall remain in that darkness for a space. All we can do is to reach out in the darkness in love and longing until in God's own good time we perceive a glimmer of light far away in the distance, as it were at the end of a tunnel, and gradually a new, more adequate image of God begins to form.

The process is summarized in a beautiful, too little-known prayer by George Appleton, which runs thus:

O Christ, my Lord, again and again I have said with Mary Magdalene, 'They have taken away my Lord and I know not where they have laid him.'

I have been desolate and alone.

And you have found me again, and I know that what has died is not you, my Lord, but only my idea of you, the image which I have made to preserve what I have found, and to be my security.

I shall make another image, O Lord, better than the last. That, too, must go, and all successive images, until I come to the blessed vision of yourself, O Christ, my Lord.

It has been suggested that the capacity to hang on in times of darkness (cognate, perhaps, with the days in the tomb?) has something to do with the capacity to find new creative solutions, a space in which to make things new when the world loses its familiar shape.

The director will discover considerable variations among directees in the extent to which they believe God to be involved in the processes of their life. Some would seek to restrict the area of their Christian faith to their private lives, and see no relevance of God to changing the structures of society or doing what we can to reduce the monumental injustice and inequality of the world. When this attitude of 'privatized' Christianity crops up I find I cannot do other than refute it absolutely, as being a travesty of the whole gospel. Some of the views expressed are so clearly contrary to Christian teaching that they need to be stoutly contradicted – and in my view this is one of them: either it is *all* God's world, *all* his concern, or it is not God's world at all.

But in other areas there may be more debatable views of God's concern over our decisions. It seems unlikely that God would be concerned (to take a ludicrous example) about what colour tie I put on in the morning. For some Christians *everything* that happens appears to revolve around *them* and *them* alone. It matters not that farmers may be desperate for rain: a fine day for their own garden party is seen as divine favour to them person-ally. I sometimes find it hard not to be a bit cynical when people 'praise the Lord' for happenings which may be very comfortable for them but diminishing or disastrous for many others.

But questions of discernment inevitably figure very promi-nently in spiritual direction: 'Is this course of action what God wants us to do or is it just our own wishes?' The decision is not helped by the opposite, somewhat masochistic view – common in some Christians – that if a decision is pleasing or advantageous to us it cannot be God's will, because God (it is implied) would only want us to do things that are unpleasant or unacceptable or that mean our giving up something.

There really are no short-cuts in these areas of discernment, which raise the problem of what are the criteria by which Christians make *any* kind of moral decision, an area in which theories are legion. Away from the rarified atmosphere of the lecture-room, in face-to-face discussion with another person, it is hard to do other than check how far various factors have been taken into account and help to assess the weight to be given to each. The director is not there to instruct people what to do, but may often help them to greater awareness of all the factors involved: e.g.

1) Is the proposed action loving? (The famous words inscribed at Mahatma Gandhi's place of cremation may sometimes be relevant: 'Recall the face of the poorest and the most helpless man whom you have seen, and ask yourself if the step you contemplate is going to be of any use to him. Will he be able to gain anything by it? Will it restore him to control over his own life and destiny?')

2) How does the proposed action respond to our *reasoning* about it?

3) How do others, whose views we respect, feel about it?

4) Does it impinge favourably or unfavourably upon the basic direction of Scripture or any major traditions of the Church?

5) What will be the consequences of acting or not acting in this way?

6) How far has the person prayed about the decision?

I confess to being less than happy with the famous Ignatian test of evaluating a decision by our inner movements of desolation and consolation over time. Many decisions which eventually prove to have been good decisions, seem to produce nothing but 'desolation' at the time of decision-making, and often it is only after the decision has been made that we feel any sense of 'consolation' at all, as we begin to come to terms with its consequences. For some, intuition may be a better guide than 'consolation' or 'desolation', but this, too, needs checking out with our other criteria.

This question of 'consolation' and 'desolation' in decision-making leads us towards the area of 'experience', which will figure largely in discussion with some directees. We are happily

41

moving out of a 'head-dominated' phase of religion with its desiccated approach to prayer and worship which could attract only intellectuals. But it may be that the awareness of feelings and emotions, and our more uninhibited responses both to other people and to God, can now make spiritual life difficult for those who genuinely do respond most readily at an intellectual level. My guess is that primarily 'feeling' people can with some effort understand how primarily 'thinking' people function, but that it is much harder for the 'thinking' ones to empathize with the 'feeling' ones, whom they are likely to perceive as irrational, or too emotional or intense.

Be that as it may, the problem of religious experience remains, and simply because of the current cult of experience, those who have little experience of God in their prayer or in their daily lives are likely to feel left out in the cold, while those who begin their Christian lives with very deep experiences of God may feel frightened and bereft if they find they no longer have such experiences.

The director will need to be able to reassure anxious people that experience is no test of the validity of a period of prayer, and that while we shall be grateful for good times in prayer and in worship, we are not to *seek* for experiences. The keynote is faithful perseverance even in times of darkness, when prayer may seem a pointless endeavour and all we seem to have done is to have offered God a bit of our time.

Nevertheless, having said this, nearly all of us go around God's world most astonishingly unaware of what surrounds us, and it seems reasonable to suppose that if we learn to become more aware of the world we shall also become more aware of God's presence in it and in our own lives. Simple awareness exercises – body awareness, awareness of breathing, awareness of the room or the garden in which we are sitting, going back over each day and trying to become aware of all the occasions where God has been at work around us and in others – all these will be helpful to most people. Our actual prayer time may well feel dry and dead, but I would suggest that if we nonetheless persevere in that prayer time, there will emerge a much more acute awareness of God at work around us in the rest of the day.

To put in another way: we may well have times when in our prayer we experience a deep and rewarding sense of peace. For this we shall be grateful, but the prayer time is no less valid and valuable if we find it a time of turmoil and anxiety and distracting thoughts. The aim of prayer is not, primarily, to have nice feelings of peace, but to be helped to *embody* peace, to *be* peaceful people out in the world.

The objective of prayer and the objective of spiritual direction therefore lies not in experience but in service. Again and again the director will come back to the touchstone, 'by their fruits you shall know them.' Far from being an esoteric, inward-looking enterprise, spiritual direction is a valuable tool in the establishment of the Kingdom, for with spiritual growth comes greater insight, and with insight comes a greater awareness of how far short of the Kingdom our world falls. As Kenneth Leech has argued cogently in *Soul Friend* and elsewhere, there is a social and political dimension to spiritual direction.

This view may encounter resistance from some who – I believe mistakenly – still see spiritual direction as cultivating hothouse blooms in the garden of the soul. But resistance is no stranger to the spiritual director. A measure of toughness and readiness to confront without fear is a seldom-stated requirement. I recall many years ago when I was training to be a marriage guidance counsellor, the tutor to the group stopped the discussion, gazed round at us, and said quite happily, 'You're a hard lot!' In following up this remark it emerged that we were all rather pleased to have been called hard, and would have been upset to have been called soft! I know that many of the times when I have let clients down, both in counselling and in direction, have been when I failed for one reason or another to challenge sufficiently toughly. To challenge is not the same as to be directive; it is to confront another person with views and ideas and feelings they have resisted looking at, and be ready to face their hostility and aggression.

It may seem strange to anyone embarking on spiritual direction, but resistance to God's action on us is characteristic of us all. Some sessions may consist in the directee trying to evade any relating of his or her life to God. Sometimes God may be implicit behind the discussion, and that is all right; but resistance and evasion need to be challenged and if possible understood. I am increasingly coming to believe that a great deal of human prayer time is devoted to resisting confrontation with God. I think it was Dr Frank Lake who once observed that most corporate worship seems to be designed by schizoid clergy to spare congregation and clergy the pain of having to meet each other. In the same way, a great deal of what we call prayer – words, Bible study, various 'techniques' – can all too easily be unrecognized devices for sparing us the difficult task of facing the reality of God himself. Spiritual direction is partly about helping people to overcome their resistance and evasion and try to face God directly.

6 Resources in Direction

I have said elsewhere that I consider the quality of the relationship between director and directee to be of primary importance. However much we fail, we are aiming for a relationship which is as close as we can achieve in similarity to God's relationship with us: loving, listening, accepting, forgiving, honest, open, not afraid of speaking the truth in love as far as that truth can be borne at the time. ('I have many things to say to you but you cannot bear them now.')[1]

The purpose of this chapter is to help us realize that there are many aids to direction over and above the direction relationship; but only the director's own developing relationship with God, combined with loving sensitivity to others and hard-won experience of directing others makes it possible to discern what is right to offer to any particular person at a particular time.

We shall therefore summarize, in alphabetical order, some thirty of the aids to direction which can be brought into use as well for the director as for those being directed. Some may appear childishly obvious, but I believe directors frequently fail to make use of the potential which lies within the most obvious and the most familiar:

Baptism
More could be made of encouraging directees to ponder over the significance of their baptism – their incorporation into Christ, their one-ness with all other Christians, their daily dying into the Cross and the indwelling Holy Spirit.

Bible
As Walter Wink has argued cogently in his *Transforming Bible Study*[2] many Christians have been put off individual study of the Bible, because of a totally head-based and academic presentation of it that is often more concerned with its literary history than its relevance to life. This not only makes the ordinary reader childishly dependent upon a presumed 'expert' having to explain what a passage really means; it ignores the genuine heart and feeling response of the ordinary reader to any passage, a response which is valid and in which lay people may need to have their confidence built up. Within direction readers can be helped

to trust their own responses to Scripture, and be shown how to interpret its teaching for themselves in their daily lives.

Body awareness

It seems reasonable that the more aware we become of ourselves as created by God, the more likely we are also to be aware of the reality of God. A good starting point, even for enquirers, is to work on simple awareness of the body God has given us, not least as a help to treating our bodies responsibly and lovingly, a not insignificant part of spiritual direction.

Breathing

Attention to breathing is also an aid to awareness, and a way of quietening the mind and body and stilling distractions. Directors need to help people to realize that we need time to *prepare* for prayer before we begin praying.

Calendar of saints

The 1980 Alternative Service Book has provided English Anglicans with a much more helpful calendar of saints, right up to more recent times, to catch our imagination. If the person of Jesus at times seems remote to some directees, attention to the saints may show one facet of the glory of Christ and help people to find him more real again. For some the person of Jesus is not easy as a focus of devotion, and to ponder the paths of the saints may be a helpful step on the way towards devotion to the person of Christ.

Church's year

Boredom is one of the great barriers to prayer, and just as the variety of the saints can light up the words of the Eucharist in many different ways, so can the variety of moods of the church year, not forgetting the profound way in which the feeling of its different stages echoes the changing atmosphere of the seasons of the natural world. Linking the liturgical year with the natural seasons can be a connection of great power for those able to make it.

Contemplative prayer

Many people use this term very loosely these days, to distinguish the prayer of quietening down from the prayer of active imagination. Suffice it to underline here that this simple quietening down prayer is not so much an advanced stage in prayer as a way of praying suitable for certain temperaments from quite early stages. Because any form of contemplation has in the past been regarded as rather 'advanced', directors need to beware of a certain spiritual pride in directees which may push some into a way of praying not really suited to them, or lead others to become discouraged because for them it never seems to come alive. Some Christians will find 'said' prayers their path to God for the whole of their lives, and need not feel that they are for that reason 'failures' in prayer: it is simply a matter of temperament.

However, it is important that those who follow a path of simple contemplative prayer should back this up with a disciplined pattern of liturgical worship and Bible study or other Christian reading. The unstructuredness and ultimate 'image-lessness' of contemplative prayer needs grounding in a sound grasp of Christian doctrine and practice if it is not to risk degenerating into the slightly dotty.

Confession

This has been referred to elsewhere. For my own part I find it hard to improve on the old Anglican adage, 'All may, none must, some should', though if we are hearing the confession of others we need to be under the discipline of confession ourselves. Too frequent confession often means over-attention to trivia and an inability to see the wood for the trees. Moreover, those who have experienced the helpfulness of informal confession may feel it stilted and artificial to return to formal confession in which there is little true meeting between penitent and confessor. Informal confession does not inhibit but rather enhances awareness of the Holy Spirit standing between penitent and confessor.

Corporate worship

A frequent problem in direction is dissatisfaction or boredom with public worship. We must occasionally acknowledge that some public worship is quite dreadful, and that boredom may be an indication for the directee to throw a few bombs around. On the other hand, boredom may denote some kind of resistance to God which needs exploring. Or people may be nostalgic for 'nice feelings' experienced in the past but no longer present. The trouble in this case is not the public worship itself, but that the directee needs to grow away from an early dependence on 'nice feelings in church'. Let us be grateful for joy in worship when it happens, but remember that 'liturgy' means 'work' – something we *do* for God and *offer* to God.

Corporate worship is important in helping the withdrawn or introverted into an awareness of the importance of the social dimension of Christianity, the strength of Christians standing together, and the need to witness publicly. Well-ordered corporate worship can be (but sadly often is *not*) one of the most all-round methods of teaching the Christian Way.

Dreams

Directees may sometimes bring dreams to the director, and these are a neglected path to the deeper and more vulnerable parts of ourselves. Unless a director has some training and support in this area, however, it is wise to be sparing in attempting to interpret. People can be helped simply by telling their dreams out loud, and directees may be invited to say whether a dream seems to be saying something to them. If a meaning strikes the director – as it frequently will – that interpretation must never be forced on the directee, but merely offered tentatively for consideration: 'I wonder whether it might be saying something like this . . . ?'

Family

Sensitivity is needed, both as to the limitations a family may place upon a directee's life and the family's capacity to help. This is quite a tricky area. Sensitivity is essential with mothers subject to the demands of small children: but even they may reasonably be challenged to find, say, ten minutes' quiet somewhere in the day.

Mental and family tensions often crop up, and even for trained counsellors it is not always easy to know how far to go into these areas. There may simply not be the time in the director's diary. On the other hand, a short burst of weekly sessions may help. A common anxiety in young parents is about getting angry with their children, and this calls for some basic putting right of misconceptions. Anger is not always wrong, and can be put to

48

good use. We are angry with what is wrong, not with the person: as the Desert Father Evagrius put it, it is always a waste of good anger to get angry with a *person*!

Awareness of the dynamics of the family is important (atheist husbands abound, and Christian belief and observance can be a lasting cause of friction), but where there is more than one Christian in the family ways can be explored of their helping each other to grow in the faith. Many couples find it hard, even when both are practising Christians, to share much of their faith together; at the other end of the scale some say they don't need to talk with anyone *but* each other. In general, though, partners are often too close to each other and lack the objectivity which a spiritual friend or director can offer.

Fantasy

Escapist fantasy, if prolonged, is of course harmful, because it has no basis in fact and prevents our facing up to the reality of life (what I'd do if I won the football pools . . . ! sexual fantasy . . . power fantasies). Fantasy can, however, be a useful tool for spiritual growth (what do I most want? . . . if everything were possible what would I like to do with my life?). Freedom from the constraints of reality for a while may help us to understand our true nature – perhaps we shall find as we fantasize that we turn out better than we had imagined, in that we'd really like to do something more public-spirited with our lives. Or we may recognize that deep down we are more self-indulgent or slothful than we had realized. To fantasize may also provide us with some kind of an ideal if it is undertaken in prayer. We may never *reach* our ideal, but it may give us the course to set, and a new direction. Ideals are like the stars: we never reach them, but we set our course by them.

The forceful reappearance of Ignatian Spiritual Direction and books like Charles Elliot's *Praying the Kingdom*[3] provide ample exploratory ground for helpful imaginative fantasy. Contemplatives who may not be much at home in the imagination will do well to explore a way that may not come easily to them, and to persevere in it for a while; but they will in the end probably find that the imaginative work 'gets in the way' between themselves and God. For others it is a helpful path *to* prayer.

Groups

Some Christians have found their main source of spiritual direction in group activity. This may be a matter of chance for some: others do find it easier to learn in groups than in a one-to-one session. In a group one can withdraw and ponder for a while, letting the others take the centre of the stage. And some can remain quiet in a group, who might find the close confrontation of one-to-one disturbing.

The greatest dangers in a group (and not only in the context of direction) are firstly the pressures towards group conformity. 'The group feels', it may be thought, when in reality several members of the group are feeling totally the opposite, but are not strong enough to counteract the powerful group pressure to conform. In some groups such pressure can be almost demonic, and it is a good group indeed that really allows lovingly for the differences of its members.

The second danger is that of a dominating, manipulating group leader, but this is no more than the danger of a dominating manipulating 'director' in one-to-one work! – except that if the majority of the group is carried along with a powerful leader, it becomes even harder to dissent.

In a more general sense the 'director' will frequently suggest membership of a prayer group, study group or other group as a way of growing in the faith.

Journalling

While this is nowadays closely linked with the work of Ira Progoff, who has introduced systematic and very releasing ways of journalling,[4] we should perhaps remind ourselves that many people kept journals before the arrival of Progoff! Some direc-tees will find it helpful to be encouraged to write, not necessarily a daily journal, but just putting something down on paper to get their thoughts and imagination flowing freely. Sometimes (though more often in counselling) I invite people to try to write down experiences which as yet they find too painful to talk about. The writing begins to release the pain, so that eventually they are freed to talk of it. Yet another use of writing is with people we feel 'could do better', who don't seem to be working hard enough or realizing their potential. To sit down with pen and paper rather than simply think or pray can be an aid to concentration and productivity.

Progoff, unfortunately a rather prolix writer, should be consulted for specific exercises, and one or two suggestions are offered in Chapter 9 below.

Laying-on of hands

In practice I have used the laying-on of hands much less frequently than I might have expected, and I wonder whether this is the experience of other directors? May it be that direction is already linked in some instances with the sacramental act of Confession? May it be that the awareness of God in the one-to-one session is already very acute, so that no further sign seems needed? Yet where there has been sickness or disturbance or unhappiness it would seem an appropriate way of ending a session, and a path that is open to lay as well as ordained directors.

Mandalas

Most directors currently at work will have been conditioned by our Western (and Protestant) obsession with words, and our blindness to visual signs and symbols. But many younger directees, in particular, will be much more open to the 'eye-gates'. To use, and perhaps to design, a mandala will be helpful for some, both as a focus for concentration and, in the case of a home-made mandala, a gathering together of ultimate concerns.

Mantras

In general I feel that it is safer to use as mantras a word or words of Christian content, rather than simply sounds to hold the concentration. If we are going into the depths where there may be dragons it is prudent to have a word or words of Scripture to accompany us.

Music

The use of music in SPIDIR courses in Spiritual Direction has made it clear that responses to it differ widely. Some people find any music a distraction; others are more selective, finding some music a barrier and other music a help. If people are easily distracted I believe that appropriate music can be a real help in quietening the mind and being open to God. This is a sort of background or 'wallpaper' use of music; for a smaller number, concentration on the music itself will be a way to God. The important thing is to recognize that prayer is a far wider activity that most directees imagine. I recall a Cathedral organist who, when asked if he would take a half-hour slot in a cycle of prayer in the Cathedral, acknowledged the problems he had in praying, and asked whether it would be an acceptable form of prayer if he played the Cathedral organ for half an hour.

Myers-Briggs personality type indicator

We have found the Myers-Briggs personality test so important on the Spiritual Direction courses that we have tried to encourage all participants to go on a basic course. It was first brought to this country by the Sisters of Emmaus House, Bristol,[5] though courses are increasingly appearing in the timetables of retreat houses and conference centres.

There is really no substitute for attending a course, though a simplified self-administered test appears in *Please Understand Me*.[6] This book provides a helpful introduction, though it excludes the very important area of the Shadow, for which reference could be made to Isabel Briggs-Myers' book *Gifts Differing*.[7]

Initially, many people are sceptical of the Myers-Briggs test, as it appears to put everyone into one or other of sixteen personality-type pigeon-holes. In reality the Indicator is much more subtle. Based on Jung's understanding of personality it recognizes, for example, that we are (to take one particular aspect) either extroverts or introverts. We may be slightly or highly one or the other; we may use *both* approaches to the world. If we are extroverts, while we need to have time alone, we shall gain renewal and vitality from being with other people. If we are introverts, while we do need contact with other people, we shall find being with others, except for one or two very close friends or relatives, a draining and demanding experience, so that we need some time alone to regather our vitality.

There are many other differences, not least in the way that extrovert and introvert people respond to different paths in spirituality, prayer and public worship.

A second way in which we differ, according to Jung and Myers-Briggs, is in whether we prefer to respond to the world primarily through our thinking processes or our feeling processes. That is not to say that 'feeling' people are unintelligent or cannot use their brains; it does mean that their preferred way of operating is through their feelings. Likewise, a 'thinking' person is not without emotion and feelings; but more frequently *prefers* to work things out logically and rationally. This means that 'feeling' people may sometimes consider 'thinking' people to be cold and heartless, while 'thinking' people may sometimes consider 'feeling' people to be over-emotional and irrational. 'Feelers' would argue that the heart has its own logic. We all use both ways at different times, and the degree to which one side or the other dominates will vary from person to person, or within the same person at different stages of their life.

Again, the pattern of prayer appropriate to a 'thinking' person will differ from the path which is helpful to a 'feeling' person.

The standard book on how our personality type affects our spirituality is Chester and Norrisey's *Prayer and Temperament*.[8]

Once we know our own type and have become familiar with the main characteristics of other basic personality types, not only shall we be able to understand much better how they respond and why they behave in the ways they do, differently from ourselves, we shall also become more sensitive to how other types of person can find the most helpful path of prayer.

Natural world

There has been much narrow-minded denigration of the simple nature-mysticism which is the mainspring of the sense of numinous in many who would not claim to be Christians. In working with 'outsiders' this is a good starting point, and often the basis of a genuine experience of God.

My anxiety in spiritual direction is much more about those whose Christianity is totally Jesus-centred, who fail to recognize that Christianity arose from a culture which had the wisdom to see God as the Lord of all creation and as reflected in the world he created. From this blindness to God in the natural world much of our exploitation, and squandering of its non-renewable resources has followed. A healthy spirituality must include an awareness of our dependence upon the natural world which God has created and from which we have sprung. This will have a direct influence on life-style and on many decisions at the place of work.

Daily office

For some lay directees, whose prayer pattern is helped by a clear framework and by verbal prayers, saying a daily office may be a valuable aid to growth. Some find it helpful to say the office alone; many more find the office helpful when said with others, but hard to cope with alone. I have never been able to understand why parochial clergy do not encourage more parishioners to join them on weekdays in saying matins or evensong in church. It requires sensitivity in timing to suit the work-patterns of lay people rather than the self-imposed timetable of the parish priest, but can be a support to a single-handed priest in his own saying of the office. I don't think I ever said daily evensong alone in the whole of my seven years in the parish I recently left, and sometimes as many as ten people attended on an ordinary weekday.

If more variety is needed than the ASB (let alone the BCP) provides, some may find help in the Taizé office or the Roman Catholic office of morning and evening prayer.

Directors need to be cautious of those who become obsessional about an office, as it can be a haven for the over-scrupulous ('I confess to failing to say evensong on the day I had my operation'!).

Pictures and icons

These are so much a matter of individual taste that the most directors can do is to give directees some idea of the value of pictures and icons in the life of prayer, and help them to recognize that words are not essential to prayer. Pictures are immensely valuable in helping us to get out of our head and into our hearts.

For many people the artistic value of a picture is of little consequence: the meaning, the reminder and the symbol are what matter. Those to whom artistic taste is important may find this painful, but the truth is that to others the most awful religious 'tat' can be an enormous help.

Politics

Spiritual Direction is about the whole of life: this is not the place to elaborate on Christianity and politics, but the director who is concerned about the whole person will find politics emerging in direction. It is not always easy to draw the line between the unchanging Christian duty to work for justice, peace and freedom and our own personal views as to *how* these can best be implemented; but we are sure to find ourselves directing Christians of different political persuasions from ourselves.

The Social Gospel is inescapable and may sometimes cause pain and opposition, either between director and directee, or between directees and their work situation or their political allegiance. There is no way round the Cross, and the issue of peace and justice may sometimes have to be faced in a painful way. To deny the involvement of the Church in changing society in a Christ-like direction is to deny the gospel.

Others may need supporting and strengthening if they encounter opposition at work or in their family when they stand up for what they believe to be good and true.

Reading

Reference has been made elsewhere to the value of 'Benedictine' reading as a way of praying. Directees may also find it easier to approach their theology through fiction and biography than through direct theological writing. There is also a wealth of Christian insight in stories written for children and adolescents. Some parishes have been able to establish helpful reading groups who tackle novels, drama and poetry rather than theology or Bible study. God is more readily accessible to many through the imagination than through the reason.

Relationships

'When I meet with you' wrote Thomas Merton, 'the Christ in you is able to meet the Christ in me in a way that would not have been possible had we not met.' Much of spiritual direction is to do with improving personal relationships. A great deal of sickness of body and mind is caused by relationships which have gone sour and hurts which have never been healed. Not only are our relationships a way of encountering reflections of the living Christ, but they frequently do need healing. Often courage may be called for in making the first move to heal a spoiled relationship, and the director may need to explore just *how* a broken relationship can be healed.

Relaxation

Many Christians are workaholics. This may sometimes be the result of neurotic guilt or a low self-image, both of which will need attention in the direction sessions. In others it may be a genuine enthusiasm for their Christian work, but nevertheless calling for a calming down, lest they burn out early or run themselves into the ground from ceasing to 'take in' but rather 'give out' all the time. Nor are workaholics usually aware of the problems their obsession causes to wives, husbands, children and colleagues. A workaholic incumbent can make life miserable for his curate.

There is much to be said for helping directees to an order of priorities in the time at their command which puts prayer first (if we are honest, how many of us really give prayer first place in our priorities?), and then, as a close second, *time off, relaxation*. Only then may the remainder of our time be safely given to working for God. We all need some holiday time each year, we all need a clear day off each week, or missed time off put together for a longer period of rest, and we all need some time for relaxation every day: Prayer – relaxation – work. Directees may need helping to see that they *matter* to God, to others and to themselves, and that they *need* time to stop and stare and do whatever they enjoy doing.

In the narrower definition of relaxation, to become relaxed is a valuable way into quietening down and being open to God in prayer. For some people, however, relaxation exercises lead not to greater awareness, but to torpor and sleep. It may well be that those in physically or mentally exhausting jobs actually need to sleep, and there are many worse ways of spending prayer time than in sleeping. On the other hand I find it better to suggest awareness exercises to people rather than relaxation, because awareness exercises keep us alert, while relaxing body and mind as a kind of by-product. Most of us are aware of only a tiny fraction of the marvellous bodies God has given us, and five minutes spent in becoming aware of 'lost' bits of ourselves is a good way to relax and become open to God in prayer.

Retreats and quiet days

The director needs to be sensitive to temperament. For many Christians a quiet day or a retreat will be unadulterated misery, and no service is done to such people by making them feel that somehow they *ought* to benefit from it. A painting or music-making weekend might be what they need, or the togetherness of a conference. We who live in families all too easily forget that those who live alone may well need for their spiritual growth no *more* aloneness and silence, but more togetherness and meeting.

Care is also needed in helping directees to find the right kind of retreat or quiet day for their own needs at the time. I have a horror of those dreadful quiet days which many parishes lay on (usually in the depths of winter) in freezing churches with little to stimulate the imagination or enthusiasm. Likewise, although for some people they are of considerable value, Ignatian retreats are emphatically not helpful for everybody, and the current near-obsession with Ignatian Spirituality does no good to anyone.

Sacraments

For some, daily Mass is a privilege and a delight: others, including some religious, find it frankly something of a trial to keep it alive and meaningful, and prevent familiarity from drifting into anaesthesia. Once again, it is a matter of temperament rather than the stage of spiritual development we have reached. For my own part, I need holiday time *away* from the sacrament if it is to remain alive for me the rest of the year.

While I believe that Quakers are misguided in their rejection of 'the' sacraments, I believe they have a great deal to tell us when they remind us that anything or anybody can be 'a' sacrament. Too narrow a concentration on 'the' sacraments can blind Christians to the presence of Christ anywhere and everywhere, lighting up the drabness of the everyday world. Directors need great sensitivity in discussing with directees the frequency with which they attend the Eucharist.

For the over-scrupulous it may well be worth thinking of the many parts of the world where it simply is not possible to receive communion more than a few times a year. The real question is how to 'use' the Eucharist (if I can put it this way without irreverence) in such a way that it is most meaningful to the directee.

Service

Christian faith needs earthing. The director will sometimes encounter those 'other worldly' Christians who are all too ready to spend long hours in prayer, but oddly disconnected from the material world of the Incarnation or from practical involvement with their fellow Christians. Baron von Hügel, in directing Evelyn Underhill, author of a once-famous work on mysticism, was insistent that she kept her feet on the ground with a practical programme of concern for the sick and the poor. We are likely to encounter resistence, but Christian wholeness cannot be reached without our feet on the ground.

For others it may be important to help them to disengage from hyperactivity, and find (at least in the second half of their lives) a still, quiet centre within. If the director is also a counsellor there are plenty of issues worth exploring with the hyperactive.

Tertiaries and oblates

The motives of directees wishing to become tertiaries or oblates of religious orders need looking at fairly objectively: there is nothing very healthy about trying to ape a romantic vision of the religious life by a sort of process of osmosis.

On the other hand, linking with one of the religious orders can be an incentive to prayer, add a sense of belonging to something bigger than ourselves, and help us to keep our own simple rule of life. The important (and difficult) point is to find the Order which is most in tune with the spirituality of the directee, but nothing is greatly lost should there be one or two false starts before finding the right one.

For the isolated and lonely there may be meetings and groups and services in the bigger orders which help to develop the sense of belonging.

Work

It is implicit in the standpoint of this book that God is the God of the whole world, and the place of work is of concern to God, not so much as a field for evangelism (though it may offer opportunities for this), but in so far as the organizations people work for are advancing or hindering the kingdom of God. This means concern as to whether working conditions contribute to the dignity, well-being and mutual respect of employees, or oppress and exploit them. We are here moving into the area of industrial mission, but only a handful of the larger businesses are touched by industrial chaplains, so directors may well find themselves being used as a sounding board for people's moral dilemmas at work.

The essential issue is how far in any individual situation Christians are to go along with what is happening (and so perhaps get their hands dirty, run the risk of compromise, and appear to be no different from anybody else), or to stand by strict principles (and so perhaps lose the chance of influencing anyone, and quite possibly lose their job). The director needs to be both sensitive to the extreme pressures of work and realistic about what is possible, and at the same time to recognize that the Christian will in some sense be different from fellow workers, an irritant and an asker of difficult questions. Here again, Christians may need a great deal of encouragement and support, and there will be areas of guilt where they feel they have not lived up to what they really believe to be right.

Yoga

For many years I have toyed with the idea of including on Stewardship questionnaires such questions as 'How far are you looking after the body God has given you, and keeping it as fit as it can be in God's service?'

To keep ourselves reasonably (not obsessively) healthy, as far as lies in our capability, is a right response to the gift of our bodies which God has given us.

Some Christians treat their bodies insultingly, with poor diet, lack of sleep and exercise, overwork and general misuse. Our spiritual awareness can be heightened or impaired by the way we treat our bodies. People even into their seventies can benefit from Yoga postures and exercises. Some people are suspicious of Yoga, fearing that it will imply beliefs incompatible with Christianity. As Hatha Yoga is generally taught in Britain today, I can see no conflict. The body is helped to become relaxed and awake, and various positions are found and held which assist in our flexibility and general health. And as we become more physically healthy so we become more alive to the reality of God, and can live with a greater sense of having acted lovingly and responsibly to the bodies God has given us.

There are, of course, many other forms of physical exercise, but Hatha Yoga (as taught in evening and day classes throughout the country) had the original intention of leading in to meditation, and a short sequence of simple postures is a splendid way into our own time of Christian prayer.

7 The Place of the Retreat in Spiritual Direction

For many years I conducted retreats on behalf of the Fellowship of Contemplative Prayer. I felt, and still feel, that the pattern of those retreats represents an advance on the familiar low-key 'preached' retreat, in that they provide a lot of time for praying together in silence and an opportunity for learning more about how to pray. This solid time of praying together helps to establish a method of simple contemplative prayer which can be continued in everyday life.[1]

Yet I felt that even those Fellowship retreats were losing a golden opportunity for spiritual direction and further growth and awareness, despite the usual encouragement to retreatants to come to talk with the conductor. Where else than in retreat could there be a better or more sustained opportunity to talk through with individuals both where they are up to in their Christian pilgrimage, and also what is actually happening to them in the course of the retreat? On many retreats only a handful of retreatants bother to take the opportunity of talking with the conductor – maybe because the conductor is so withdrawn as not to inspire confidence? But I believe that a retreat could well be the starting point for many people to discover the action of God in their lives, and to start on the path of having a spiritual director.

A lot was (and is) being done by the Jesuits with their rediscovery of the individually guided retreat, and I think that all involved in the work of spiritual direction owe them a debt of gratitude for what they have done. Nevertheless, it remains a fact which the Jesuits would be the first to acknowledge, that the Ignatian Exercises are not helpful to every Christian, and also that many people come to a retreat with their own personal agenda for it already worked out, rather than wanting to be taken along a predetermined line in the Exercises. I recognize that retreatants are encouraged to take their own time in going through the Exercises, and may not reach the 'End', but it is, nevertheless, a 'set path' that the Exercises follow.

For two years after my own Ignatian experience I made wide-ranging enquiries about what might be happening in terms of one-to-one retreats along other than Ignatian lines. But it became clear that everyone involved in one-to-one retreat-giving was working to some extent along Ignatian lines, and I could discover no-one with the truly 'client-centred' approach, open to all traditions of spirituality, which I believed to be a fruitful line to pursue.

So if anything was to happen it seemed that a fool would have to rush in where others had feared to tread, and I booked a retreat house for a Monday-to-Thursday retreat, publicizing the event as widely as I could.

I was extremely fortunate at this stage to have been joined in the parish by a deaconess colleague, Dorothy Nicholson, a former health visitor. She brought from her Health Service background a different orientation to the counselling side from my own marital- and group-orientated counselling training, along with a maturity of vision and the experience of more recent learning methods on the Southwark Ordination Course. In what follows, we have worked out the approach together, and I am very grateful for this collaboration.

Any individually guided retreat unavoidably makes heavy demands on the retreat conductor's time. I reckon that six retreatants are as many as can be managed by one person on a retreat, given all the other things that have to be done, while still being able to hold each new person as an individual.

We felt there should be some shared input, so we began with a daily morning session consisting of a talk followed by discussion, and rounding off with a practical session of praying in a different way each day. For some retreatants these approaches to prayer were quite new, and were much welcomed. These morning input sessions provided a framework for those needing more 'feeding' than just the daily half-hour session with one of the retreat givers. One needs to be sensitive to the varying amount of 'input' needed by different people.

There was a daily morning Eucharist, and each day concluded with Compline by candlelight. There was no address at Compline, but recorded music and a story – on the basis that a story might well provide more possibilities for imaginative pondering during the evening than a more abstract talk.

I had previously had many years of conducting retreats, but on this first new venture what I found most startling was the fact that every person had come into the retreat with different needs, as well as a different personality pattern and a different experience of prayer. For one or two retreatants straight counselling was desperately needed, which had not been sought or found elsewhere. I think this is something which anyone involved in one-to-one retreats needs to be aware of. In an ideal world all retreat conductors and all spiritual directors should have at least a basic knowledge of counselling. And in the intensity of a retreat, conductors who do not have a counselling background at least need to be sensitive about not getting out of their depth or going beyond their ability to handle the situation. In some instances it may even be unhelpful to talk much about God directly before some more pressing matters have been at least partially resolved. God can all too easily be used as an escape.

For other retreatants, who had brought less of an agenda with them, attention could be given from the start to the actual experience of the retreat, helping them to become more sensitive to the presence of God in the present moment. A very warm response at the end of this first retreat encouraged the arrangement and conduct of further retreats along these lines. I do not think it was lightly said by two retreatants that after this kind of retreat it would be very hard to go back to an old-style 'preached' retreat. For several, it was an encouragement to look for an ongoing spiritual director.

Yet valuable as that first week was, helped by the traditional sense of 'apartness' of a residential retreat, that pattern cannot be the answer for everyone. Not all can get away for a whole week, owing to family and other commitments, by no means all can afford the expense of going away into retreat, and many mature and prayerful Christians simply cannot cope with long periods of silence.

So where were we to go from here?

Again, the Jesuits provided us with a starting point in their 'At Home' 'retreats'. But was a weekly meeting over a thirteen-week period in any sense a *retreat*? Where was the connected concentration of a retreat? Was it not – however valuable – more of a *course* than a *retreat*? And if it took people along a largely pre-determined path was it allowing as much freedom as it might for differing individual needs?

We felt that some people might find more value in exploring a very different path, or in pursuing the same path in a different direction.

We therefore made a second experiment, this time parish-based, in which we invited participants (again limited to twelve, though ten would have been better) to continue their normal life over a Monday-to-Friday period, but to cut out everything inessential so as to give as much time as possible to prayer and reflection.

The commitment we asked for was for a morning session, when we again provided some input, this time tracing different ways of experiencing and relating to God as we grow up through childhood to adulthood and maturity, a theme which seemed particularly appropriate for a group consisting predominantly of mothers with growing children. As on the residential retreat the short talk was followed by discussion and by a period of prayer of different kinds.

Each retreatant had a daily half-hour (usually longer) one-to-one session with one of the conductors. On this occasion the conductors travelled round to retreatants, but for future occasions it was resolved that wherever practicable retreatants should come to the conductor, since the week proved very demanding. It became clear that it was easier in theory than it was in practice to shut off all other parish commitments. The only other happening we asked all retreatants to come to was a house Communion on the Friday evening, followed by a wine and cheese party during which we were able to share some of the week's experiences and receive the predominantly positive feed-back. This also provided a chance to unwind a bit and re-enter the ordinary world.

For those who wished, we laid on candelit Compline in church each evening, happily attended by some non-retreatants as well, and there was also available, of course, the usual round of daily Evensong and weekday Eucharists.

There can be no doubt that this was an important event – indeed for several people quite decisive for growth or major change of direction. Those with experience of 'preached resi-dental' retreats commented that although the sense of quietness and apartness was to some extent missing, the timetable made it a very concentrated period, in which real attention could be given to the immediacy of God. For some it was the first time that God had been seriously thought about, spoken about or experienced in the everyday realm of ordinary family and home events. It could well have been called an important piece of spiritual direction, and has borne lasting fruit in the readiness of those who came to it to talk to each other about things that matter, and to return subsequently to talk to the conductors. The event was also largely instrumental in the formation both of a continuing discussion group and of other more ad hoc meetings on important topics.

This experiment – again repeated and into the regular diary – helped to include some for whom an away-retreat was either impossible or, on past experience, unhelpful. But it still did not include everybody who wanted some kind of experience of retreat, and more particularly, of an individually guided one.

It was not long before the expected question was actually asked: 'That's all very well, but what about those of us who have to go out to work during the day?'

At first the venture seemed impracticable in terms of timing, quite apart from the question of how far such an experiment could be called a retreat. But as the demand continued, a Monday-to-Friday period was provisionally set aside in the church diary.

Yet how to fit it in? In a fairly leafy commuter belt, people have to leave for work quite early in the morning. We could hardly run a 6.30–7.30 a.m. input session and expect people to come; and for some, even this would not have been early enough.

So we settled for a strictly timetabled evening input hour, 8–9 p.m.: fifteen minutes talk, twenty minutes discussion, twenty-five minutes prayer each evening. We included the now well-established house Communion and wine and cheese party on the Friday, and managed to fit in the pivotal one-to-one sessions in the early morning, early evening or late evening.

While personal agendas were again as varied as ever, what was most striking about this retreat was the way that the reality of God was brought to bear upon everyday work situations, upon moral dilemmas at work, upon personal relationships, upon questions of authority and leadership. For some, it was quite startling and new to recognize the closeness and the relevance of God to the whole of life, and again there has been very real growth in the Spirit and a new openness.

As I explained at the beginning of this chapter, this work is very demanding of staff time, but I believe the growth and realization of latent potentiality worth this expenditure. I think it is no coincidence, but because over the years we have tried in the parish to give generous amounts of *time* to people, that we have experienced something of a 'ministry explosion'. And as the ministry team has grown, so those ministers have themselves become instruments of the Spirit in helping *others* to grow and realize their own God-given potentiality. The work of leading these home-based retreats is itself something which can be shared more widely as we begin to locate those with the necessary sensitivity for this kind of ministry. Above all, these retreats have introduced a whole new range of people to spiritual direction. We have recently instituted a follow-up session six months after home-based retreats, and this has reinforced our realization of the value of these ventures, not only in establishing people in a healthy and non-dependent direction relationship, but in enabling them to recognize the need and value of someone with whom to talk things through. For others the value was different: 'The most important week in my life' . . . 'For the first time I was taught to pray properly' . . . 'It got me going on regular daily prayer' . . . 'I learned three things – that God loves us just as we are, it helped to establish the person of Jesus for the first time, and I realized the value of ''being'' as distinct from ''doing''.'

I am sure there must be other experiments of this kind going on in the country which I have not heard about, and I should be grateful to discover anything that is happening, because briefer published reports of what we have been doing, while they have attracted a lot of interest, have not so far uncovered news of any similar ventures.

The following list of themes we have used on both residential and home-based retreats may be of interest to some readers. On a short retreat it is hard to improve on variants long established:

Death,

Resurrection,

The new life of faith.

For retreats directed primarily to people at work, the addresses and following discussion have flourished with some such sequence as:

God in Time (everyone, it seems, has a problem with their time; Michel Quoist observed, years ago, 'there is always time for what God wants us to do'),

God in Weakness, and

God in Power (most retreatants experience both weakness and power in their work situations),

God in Structures.

Symbols or images of the Christian life are valuable – they are legion, but, for example:

Shepherd,

Desert-Dweller,

Soldier,

Messenger,

Prophet.

In using images of this kind we found it helpful to point out that all images have a shadow side, a fact so often forgotten by enthusiastic Christians. The Pilgrim may have an inability to sit still or to stay with a problem and wrestle with it, the desert dweller may tend to deny the material world and the potential goodness of the senses, the messenger can all too easily become the hot-gospelling bigot with an imagined hot-line to God. The Soldier can become over-much the conserver of tradition, too much the believer in worldly power and unable to relate to valuable female ways of dealing with a situation, while the Shepherd needs to be wary of becoming a smotherer and a paternalistic do-gooder.

I come back repeatedly, however, to inviting retreatants to consider the stages of growth briefly outlined elsewhere in this book, including the way in which our understanding of God develops as we mature. The value of this lies partly in the way it helps during the retreat to uncover important half-forgotten formative events, both good and bad, which can be either healed or used to energize the present:

Birth, infancy, childhood,

Adolescence,

Young Adulthood,

The Middle Years,

Eventide.

8   Direction and the 'Outsider'

For some, this chapter may hardly come within the boundaries of spiritual direction, if the term spiritual direction is only to be used for an ongoing relationship with a professing Christian.

I should wish to disagree with this view. In the SPIDIR network as a whole, and especially in the courses for spiritual directors, we have time and again encountered concern not only for spiritual direction, as such, in its standard 'contracted' form, and not only for the valuable one-off encounters with practising Christians where quite suddenly and unexpectedly we would find ourselves deep in discussion about their relationship with God. We have also had repeated questions about similar encounters with those who profess a minimal Christian faith or are simply honest enquirers. If this be seen as more appropriately classified as 'apologetics', or 'pastoral care' or 'outreach', so be it; to me it seems to be an important branch of spiritual direction, however brief or peripheral.

The first consideration is the stance of the Christian to whom the 'outsider' addresses the question. For some the answer is coloured by a simple unashamed desire to obtain a convert, and to press the Christian case in season and out. Whether this approach really allows the enquirer – already at a disadvantage with an informed Christian – the genuine freedom which I believe God gives to all of us, is at least debatable. I should myself prefer to leave enquirers feeling free to accept or reject in their own time. I can only be what I am – a Christian; but a true personal relationship is always a two-way learning process. I should feel myself lacking in integrity if I did not enter into every discussion prepared to change my own mind about quite basic beliefs, should I be convinced by my questioner: to do less would be to treat them as less than a person. I feel strongly about this because of all too many encounters with blinkered and narrow Christians who echo that familiar desk-sign, 'Don't confuse me with facts: I've made up my mind.'

However, most outsiders or nominal Christians who seek direction from known Christians will already have certain assumptions about where we stand. Most probably they come because a friend who has already been to talk with us, and found us in some sense trustworthy or helpful, has told them about us.

The essence of our response will be love and respect for another of God's children, whether or not we speak of God directly. If they come with a problem to present, we must give our primary attention to that problem, not attempt to press them towards Christian belief. I could not disagree more strongly with the view of Jay Adams, highly influential in the United States, who argues that there is no real value in counselling anyone till they have become a professing Christian. I do not detect this narrow attitude in the way Jesus responded to the sick or distressed.

In direction as in counselling, the presenting problem sometimes bears little relationship to the real problem. Just as the general medical practitioner may be presented with a physical symptom when the real problem is stress at work or sexual disfunctioning, so the parish priest or known Christian is often presented with a 'God-problem', when the real worry may be emotional or situational.

How then do we relate to the outsider who has approached us? One of the great mistakes I believe the Churches have made in recent years has been to define the boundaries of 'belonging-or-not-belonging' much more sharply than in the past. The Parish Communion is, I am sure, the right main service of the day, but it all too easily leaves the fringe person with a sense of exclusion, in not being able to receive Communion. And a strict baptism policy, whatever its merits, leaves a large number of people feeling excluded and unwanted: 'We thought it was the right thing to have our baby baptized and now you tell us to go away.' Folk religion has been persistently derided as mere superstition, yet earlier generations would have more wisely started from where people *are*, and made popular religion a positive point of contact with 'Something Other' on which to build a more satisfying belief. However, there are signs that all is not lost (see *Breakthrough, a Work Book in Popular Religion*[1]), and that some Christians are again beginning to see how popular religion can be used positively.

When non-churchgoers come to enquire about baptism, for example, can we not work on what they already have of an awareness of God, rather than bludgeon them prematurely into attending church regularly for the next six months or whatever?

Most casual encounters are less definable than a baptism request, and the extent to which we can develop these meetings lies very largely in our own sensitivity to what is going on under the surface. A measure of such sensitivity has transformed many a boring party into a really worthwhile discussion! How often one encounters a sense of lostness, a lack of meaning or purpose, an awareness that the money-making job is unsatisfactory or even soul-destroying. 'Who are you?' 'Where are you?' 'What do you really want?' – at one level or another, these remain key questions for believer and unbeliever alike.

This kind of ad hoc spiritual ministry to outsiders tends to be more problem-centred than is the case in straight spiritual direction: problems of illness, bereavement, unemployment, moral dilemmas, sexual problems, failure in a personal relationship. It is a strange paradox that at a time when professing Christians probably seek sacramental Confession less frequently than for a long while, outsiders often demonstrate a need to 'tell someone' which is impressively honest. Confession, however informal, helps us to face uncomfortable reality. Tilden Edwards observes sagely, 'in Spiritual Direction there is a danger of focusing on some ethereal relation to God or of interior experience in ways that evade accountability for one's behaviour both for things done and undone.'[2] Maybe Christians can learn from the outsider's need to 'tell someone about it'.

What we are looking for with outsiders, I suppose, is some point of contact between where the person is and an area of Christian insight, belief or practice which could enlighten their situation. To take an obvious example, many people in the West (though fewer today than ten years ago?) have been looking to the East for forms of meditation, being unaware of the deep contemplation practised within Christianity. Since we are still having to work to open up this tradition to lifelong practising Christians, it is hardly surprising that outsiders look elsewhere for training in meditation and contemplation. They may, however, not yet be able to hear any very direct Christian teaching. And I do *mean* 'not yet able' to hear: until we are ready we simply cannot *hear*. So, rather than speak to the deaf, I prefer to trust the Holy Spirit and the intuition of enquirers, which when they *are* ready will prompt them to look for answers to the more directly Christian questions. If people are looking for ways of learning to be quiet, I do not think we should be afraid of inviting them to practise simple breathing and awareness exercises, and ways towards quietening the mind. If we can take literally the words, 'Be still and know that I am God', we may learn to trust the indwelling Holy Spirit to do the work for us. I believe those words mean precisely what they say: if we are still, we *shall* come to know God. It is as simple as that: we do not need avalanches of words and books: 'Be still and know that I am God'.

I would therefore have no hesitation (unless there were signs of mental illness or serious imbalance of some kind) in inviting any interested outsider to sit quietly in the garden or before a large window and simply try to become more aware of what they can see there, to enter into the reality of what surrounds them. Simple awareness of breathing is also invaluable in quietening the mind, not altering the pattern of breathing, but feeling the air cold as it enters the nostrils and warm as it leaves, or feeling how deep into the body the breath seems to go, and then thinking of ourselves as breathing in new life and vitality, and as having the choice of breathing out either our own selfishness or something of the new life we have just breathed in.

Simple exercises to develop awareness of the body can be suggested, and exercises in quietening the mind, in being aware of thoughts and distractions, can be suggested to believer and unbeliever alike. And if these are persevered with there are likely to arise further questions which can take us into more specifically Christian teaching – but only if there is a wish for it.

In recent years such exercises in quietening the mind have worried some people who have pointed out that many Eastern forms of meditation, and also Christian ways of teaching meditation and contemplation, focus on acquiring inner peace and quiet. They raise the objection that we are hardly entitled to go looking for personal peace and quietness in a world where there is so much injustice, hunger, poverty and warmongering aggression, and remind us that Jesus said, 'In the world you shall have tribulation.' Christians, they argue, are not justified in seeking inner peace while the world is so cruelly unjust and full of unnecessary suffering.

The dilemma recurs in Spiritual Direction, and one sees the force of both sides of the argument. I believe both are right in some degree. The Jesus who told us that in the world we shall have tribulation was the same Jesus who told us 'My peace I give you, not as the world gives.' This was not a promise for the future: it was in the present tense, a promise of Peace *now*.

As I have implied throughout this book, I do not believe that we should look for wonderful experiences in our prayer, but they may well be given to us from time to time. I *do* believe that we are meant to *express* peace in the world; and therefore to attempt in our prayer-time to enter in some way *into* that Peace seems to me to be a prior condition of knowing how to *be* peaceful people in the world. As always, the test is whether something is undertaken for our own selfish pleasure, or for the good of others. To try to be open to the Peace of God in our prayer – and maybe sometimes to find something of it – seems to me a necessary prerequisite to *taking* the peace of Christ out into the world. And honest enquirers may well be able to share this task with us.

In talking with non-Christians or nominal Christians I come back again and again to the importance of relationships. Genuine religion is about relationships with God and with each other. Formal, dead, unreal religion runs away from true relationships, hiding in stilted formalities which safeguard our prejudices and fears by distancing us from true encounters with either God or each other. Said prayers, ordered forms of worship, 'head-orientated' Bible study, ways of arranging churches and services so that we are not conscious of each other's presence – all these are means of avoiding real meetings with God and with God-in-our-neighbour.

In any human encounter we can encourage the meeting of real people. Only one party may be conscious of encountering the presence of God in the other, but even if only one is aware of the depths within each human meeting, this may bring consequences beyond anything we ever actually see. It is sad when narrow-minded Christians seem to believe that the love of God can only be expressed in verbal terms, and that words of Scripture must always be dragged in. On the contrary, the love of God can be mediated far more effectively through actions and attitudes than through words. Our basic human encounter can be a parable of our encounter with God.

That is why the personal spirituality of the spiritual director is of such importance. However inadequate and imperfect all of us may feel, ultimately it is by what we *are* rather than by what we *say* that others will be influenced. I remember many years ago as a very new and raw Christian going to stay at an Anglican monastery. I was met at the station by a monk in the monastery car. On the drive back very little was said, yet I felt very small, very inadequate and very grubby from the world. Nevertheless, I knew I was welcomed and accepted just as I was. There was no verbal preaching, but the memory of that short encounter has remained with me vividly over the years. What we *are* matters far more than what we *say*.

On the face of it this may seem obvious. Yet I am convinced that there is little, if anything, new to say about the Christian enterprise, and many on the fringes know it already in their heads, in their intellect.

What the spiritual director is concerned about, with Christian and outsider alike, is finding ways of taking what we already know in the mind down into the heart, so that it becomes a part of our deepest experience; and the *quality* of the direction relationship – of *any* relationship – is one of the most important factors in transferring our faith from head to heart. In the final analysis I believe that the most important thing in direction has relatively little to do with what is said, but a great deal to do with the quality of the relationship between director and directee.

9   Training the Directors

There may be some younger people to whom others are drawn in a search for direction, but more generally we look in a director for a quality of maturity and integration which takes time to develop. In Jungian terms, a good director needs to be aware of his or her shadow and to have come to terms with it. So it is hardly surprising that spiritual direction is not a subject for theological college training, nor (as far as I know) for post-ordination training. Traditionally, it has simply been assumed that people go for direction to someone who has certain abilities. Indeed, in SPIDIR (of which more later), when setting up a course in spiritual direction one of the difficulties we encountered was a conviction among some committee members that spiritual direction cannot be taught: that it is a gift you either have or do not have, and that consequently there was no point in running a course at all.

Eventually, as we shall see, a course did get off the ground. My own view is that there are certain qualities which make a good director: if those qualities are there, then the gift can be nurtured and developed. We have insisted that those accepted for a course must already be being used as directors by others, even if in some instances in a fairly informal way. For example, young people exploring their Christian faith are not likely to want formal pre-booked sessions; their queries will more probably be dealt with on the spot, or perhaps within some kind of a group. As indicated earlier, it is also important that if we direct others we are ourselves being directed.

I would readily agree, however, that just because someone went through a course of training, this would not entitle them, as it were, to put up a brass plate on their door as a 'qualified spiritual director'. Others would have to recognize qualities in them which they felt would help them, and of these qualities (God help us) I believe the most important is some glimmering of holiness – which indeed *cannot* be taught, but is a matter of Grace.

To list the qualities of a good director may sound not unlike the average parish cataloguing the qualities of the archangel

Gabriel, which they require to be present in their next incumbent. But apart from that glimmering of holiness and commitment to God, one is looking for a genuine and lively interest in the exciting *variety* of prayer, a readiness to experiment, and a measure of maturity and awareness of self – for someone who is unafraid of their own negative qualities like anger and pride, and not afraid either of their own sexuality or of the sexuality and strong emotions of others. A good director will in fact share many of the qualities of the good counsellor. This means an ability to listen rather than to preach and lecture (people used to walk for days on end to see one of the Desert Fathers and come away with a single sentence or maybe only a symbolic action); a readiness not to impose one's own patterns but respond to the person before us; and a warmth of personality which will encourage directees to share their difficult and unacceptable bits. It also means an awareness of our own emotional responses while still concentrating primarily on the directee; an awareness of the bewildering difference of other people; and (I feel this very strongly) an openness to share ourselves, but only insofar as it will be helpful for others, not for our own self-assertion. If Christianity is about growing into the fullness of the stature of Christ it is about wholeness, and the more whole and complete a person the director is the more effective the direction will be, and the more real humanity there will be to share in the direction relationship. This is an important point, and another area where I believe there is a difference between direction and most counselling and psychotherapy. In a strict Freudian session, the therapist (in order not to inhibit a range of projections which may be helpful in the therapy) does not really function as a whole person, but more as a mirror reflecting back to the patient. While other styles of therapy and counselling may modify such strictness, most counsellors and therapists (partly to assist the healing and partly in self-defence!) do not really function as whole people in the counselling relationship. Personal questions to the counsellor will be parried, contact outside the counselling session and certainly social contact will be discouraged in a measure of professional aloofness. (A notable exception to this stance was that of the Christian therapist Paul Tournier, who always used his own personality to the full in his work and shared the whole of himself.)

If Christianity is about wholeness and relationships, then

unless two people are genuinely meeting as whole people, there is something less than Christian about their meeting, and as time goes on I find that in both direction and counselling I am using more rather than less of myself. There are risks, of course, that the directee's confidence may be shaken with the realization of faults and weaknesses in the director, but that awareness – and acceptance – of fault and weakness is a part of any true adult and Christian relationship. For me, a meeting of two people cannot be less than the meeting of two *whole* people. In other words, a considerable part of the direction lies in the direction relationship itself.

That wholeness will extend to an awareness of feminine qualities in male directors and masculine qualities in female directors. Hurding, analysing the work of Clinebell, expresses it thus:

> At the individual level, a new freedom should be sought in what Clinebell describes as 'androgynous wholeness'. He points out that Jesus both showed characteristics that we tend to identify more with men – 'courage, strength, leadership and concern for justice' – and those we see as womanly – 'caring, compassion, tenderness, and responsiveness to the needs of others.' Clinebell declares that the Lord 'demonstrated that both sets of qualities are neither masculine nor feminine but *human* capacities' . . . The feminist movement has allowed many women to discover the more analytical and assertive sides to their nature. And yet, I have often found a deep resistance amongst male clients to acknowledge and express the more tender, nurturing, vulnerable and intuitive facets of their personalities. Such would benefit greatly, both within themselves and in their friendships, if they could let the guard slip and live out the richness of their inner selves more fully. [1]

Clinebell (talking of counselling, but relevant to our discussion) feels that men in general are unable to enter fully into the feelings of many women of today, who still feel in many respects second-class citizens, not least in the life of the Christian Church; but that as a man moves towards that 'androgynous wholeness' he would become more effective as a counsellor (or director) to women. In the meantime Clinebell makes a plea for more women counsellors.

This point of view may be compared interestingly with that of Tilden Edwards, writing specifically about spiritual directors from his wide experience of training directors at the Shalem Institute in Washington, who suggests a very real value in women directing men and in men directing women:

> Psychologically, if we accept Carl Jung's sense of the process for internal integration of anima and animus ('feminine' and 'masculine' psychic dimensions), such a relationship can be valuable. Through transference, images of femininity from my inner world are projected on to the spiritual director (reverse for a woman), who 'returns' them to me, to be integrated within my personality.
>
> In the spiritual order, we might say that qualities of the Divine lacking in my own consciousness are projected, returned and integrated. Genesis 1.27 implies that the very image of God is male and female. Scriptural imagery also reflects masculine- and feminine-associated qualities of God interacting with their opposites in people. [2]

Edwards goes on to say that if this be so it underlines the rightness of the director's generally being in the second half of life, and having reached the point of discovering that sexual intercourse is not the most important experience in life, thus freeing direction relationships for the realm of agape rather than eros. He suggests that for a really mature person (having come towards Clinebell's 'androgynous wholeness') it matters little whether the director is of the same sex or different.

My own view is initially the rather down-to-earth one that, given the present paucity in Britain of competent directors, if you can find a good director of either sex, stay there! For those who are sufficiently open there is a great deal to be gained from a cross-directing, but I am also aware that many people who seek direction are to some extent psychologically damaged, and will (at least initially) feel more at ease with a same-sex director. Nevertheless, the sooner more male Christians can come towards 'androgynous wholeness', not least through the experience of direction by a woman, the sooner the Church will lose its adolescent hang-ups about the ordination of women. Direction can lead to wholeness in the most unexpected ways!

The most serious problem is the shortage of competent spiritual directors. On all sides I hear people asking 'Who can I go to see?', and the few well-known names are already over-loaded. But the problem is not insuperable, and I believe a systematic effort could over a period of years provide an adequate number of sensitive and trained directors.

The most useful and practical way I can discuss the question of training in direction will be to trace in some detail the development of the SPIDIR network in the Anglican Diocese of Southwark over the last seven years or so, so that others may be able to use some of our ideas in a larger or smaller way, or learn from our mistakes and successes. I would hope that similar ventures may be started elsewhere.

The ultimate origin and instigators of SPIDIR are lost in obscurity, but the effective beginning was a letter sent to all clergy in the diocese inviting them to a meeting to see whether ways could be found of helping those who were involved in the spiritual growth of others. From the start, the venture had the support of the then director of Pastoral Counselling in the diocese, Canon Derek Blows, now Director of the Westminster Pastoral Foundation. This was important for the future, because SPIDIR could see itself, not as in competition with the counselling agency of the diocese (with which I was myself closely involved at the time), but as complementing it. The more secular, psychological model of counselling in the diocese left room for a network which was based primarily on the God-relationship, rather than primarily on the person-to-person relationship.

In the event, something not far short of a hundred out of about three hundred stipendiary clergy in the diocese appeared for the conference – a truly astonishing number, which showed that there was a vast area of unmet need in the diocese. However, by the end of the day it was clear that there were also about a hundred different ideas as to how the situation should develop. A second meeting was called, attended by some forty clergy, preceded by an address on spiritual direction by Gonville Ffrench Beytagh, when the way forward was still no clearer, and there seemed every likelihood that the venture would silently expire.

It was at this point that Derek Blows approached me with a view to forming and heading a committee which would take some effective action. It was, incidentally, Derek who suggested the name SPIDIR.

From the start we were emphatic that the venture should

represent all shades of churchmanship. All too easily spiritual direction might be seen as a catholic preserve, and there has always been evangelical, liberal, catholic and charismatic representation on our committee. We also recognized from the start both the ministry of women and the fact that direction is not solely a clerical preserve, so the committee has included women and other lay people.

Other dioceses or groups setting up an organization to help those involved in spiritual direction may well find it worthwhile setting up a series of regular support groups of six to twelve people. However, in Southwark, the Pastoral Counselling organization already had a highly developed network of groups to support those involved in counselling or other pastoral care, and it seemed wrong and possibly competitive to set up another network of groups more specifically concerned with spiritual direction. We were further aware that, to have any real cutting and teaching edge, each group would require a leader or leaders, who would in turn need their own support group, and in the early stages it was clear that we did not have such resources. It would nevertheless be an interesting and worthwhile venture to work on such a basis, and in a diocese or other area where no counselling and pastoral care groups exist, it could well prove that a network with spiritual direction as its primary focus could include within it some basic training in those counselling skills which are so helpful as a background to everyone involved in direction. I say this, at the risk of repetition, because counselling cannot be learned from books. At the time I also felt that more specific training was needed than the support groups and informal learning from group interaction alone could provide.

Having established our wide-ranging committee and rejected the idea of a new network of support groups, we decided that the first task was to raise the level of general awarenss of the value of and need for spiritual direction, and arouse interest in topics of help to those involved in direction. Very early on, therefore, we began publishing a newsletter, which was sent free to all incumbents and deaconesses in the diocese, and to all who attended our meetings. The SPIDIR newsletter, published three times a year, now has a production run of 2,000 copies and goes all over the country.[3]

We began our other work with a Lenten series of four sessions led by Sister Eileen Mary SLG on 'the relevance of mystical tradition to contemporary life', and, somewhat alarmed by the apparent abstruseness of the topic, booked a small room suitable for about twenty people and hoped someone other than the committee would appear. Throughout the course about forty people were packed around the walls and on the floor, and so began our continuing pattern of three day-conferences a year, open to all.

These conferences have been headed by such people as Keith Sutton, Richard Harries, Andrew Louth, Michael Marshall, Morris Maddocks, Peter Baelz, Rowan Williams, Martin Israel, Charles Elliott, John Foskett, Richard Buck and Ian Ainsworth-Smith. Attendance has not dropped below the seventy mark and has topped two hundred – all on weekdays, with a good balance of laity and clergy. The following topics have been covered so far, and there seem to be enough new topics bubbling up at every committee meeting to keep these day-conferences going on worthwhile subjects for many years to come:

Absolution Today (seen from Catholic and Evangelical stand-points)
Children, Young People and Prayer
New Directions in the Retreat Movement
The Two Languages (Theology and Psychology)
Praying Round the Clock
The Ministry of Christian Healing
Daily Prayer and Daily Office
Exorcism
Guilt
Facing Mortality
Leading Prayer Groups
Intercessory Prayer
The Anglican Spiritual Tradition
Prayer and Politics
Prayer and Human Development
The Person of Jesus in the Life of the Christian (seen from Liberal and Evangelical standpoints)
Praying the Kingdom
The Psalter

Committee members not unexpectedly found themselves in demand for leading discussion in deanery synods and chapters on the subject of Spiritual Direction, and this has been a quiet but steady means of putting direction more firmly on the map. We have also been used in clergy post-ordination and in-service training, and in the training of readers in the diocese as well as in many lay training courses. A valuable monthly reading group was sustained for several years till removals indicated that its time was over.

Valuable as this work was, and is, we were aware that it was evading the more direct task of training and supporting those actually involved, or becoming involved, in spiritual direction. So a small sub-group was deputed to try to set up a course of more systematic training. But the more the group discussed the matter the more formidable the obstacles appeared. We were working entirely without financial backing and the current ecclesiastical and educational climate looked bleak for help in either direction. The logistics of having visiting lecturers for small numbers seemed increasingly daunting, and people of different traditions within the planning group laid rather different emphases on what would best constitute the main part of the course. A helpful suggestion from Richard Garrard, Director of In-Service training in the diocese, was that rather than a multi-staffed course there might be some mileage in the age-old tradition of a group gathering round a wise leader – a sort of guru – and learning in very simple ways from such a person and from each other.

The only difficulty was the apparent absence of neighbour-hood gurus, or at least of any suitable person with the time to spare for such a venture. Increasingly, it looked as though the main purpose for which SPIDIR had been formed would fall by the wayside.

The only solution seemed to be a group without a guru which would formulate its own course according to the needs of its members. For some time I had felt I should be handing over the chairmanship of SPIDIR to someone else; so Rodney Bomford, who had been on the committee from the start, succeeded me as chairman, and I undertook to try to get a training course off the ground. I want now to spell out in a little detail how this developed since other courses do seem likely to be set up elsewhere, and our experience may be of value. I shall then outline some of the types of activity on the courses which could be of interest not only for similar courses but also for one-off training ventures at diocesan or more local level.

A guru might be unavailable, but a course would still need some direction, and I have been helped in this by years of experience in counselling, and in small group work and supervision of others engaged in pastoral work. I was able to discuss in person some of the work being done in spiritual direction courses in New York, and have found Tilden Edwards' book *Spiritual Friend* invaluable in its account of the formation of the Washington course. There has also been liaison with the staff of Heythrop College over the experimental early years of their Jesuit course in spiritual direction, and I have been grateful for this help. The late Martin Thornton opened up in correspondence many important questions, and the Association for Promoting Retreats has been running short courses in Bristol. Other than these I have not so far been able to locate any ventures in systematic training in England.

It seemed paramount to achieve a balance of head and heart, of theoretical and experiential learning, absence of the latter being one of my worries about Martin Thornton's course. A pattern was therefore evolved, which has stood the test of time, of meeting once a month for a year from 10.30 a.m. to 3.30 p.m. Sessions start promptly, as course members are busy people, with half an hour of prayer led by one of the members. Each month a different sort of prayer is explored, and each month's lecture session, if it so lends itself, is appropriately echoed in the following month's prayer session. We have tried to give attention not only to the more obvious methods of prayer, but to symbols, movement, and other activity including music. Music, in particular, has aroused a lot of discussion, and it has become clear that responses to music used in prayer are so varied that a great deal of care and caution needs to be given if some people are not to be distracted and put off rather than helped by it. Time is always given to discussion after the prayer session. Trying to assess a time of prayer in this way may sound a little clinical, and we are aware of this, but such discussion – being quite frank about what has been helpful and what has not – has been of inestimable value, enabling members to recognize how widely differing are the responses of others to the same stimuli. It has been one of the most worthwhile things we have done, and has helped members to be far more sensitive in listening to their own directees' responses and needs, and to avoid suggesting ways of praying that would be totally unsatisfactory. Directees are sometimes too polite to complain, and not as forthright as course members have become as they have grown together.

Chester and Norrisey's *Prayer and Temperament*[4] and of course, Anthony di Mello's *Sadhana*[4] and *Wellsprings*[5] are good source-books for varied kinds of prayer. Una Kroll's *Spiritual Exercise Book*[6] is also good in its use of symbols. Christian prayer has been obsessed by *words* and therefore all too easily with *head* learning to the detriment of the heart. But a very large number of people simply do not respond readily to words, whereas symbols and visual aids can be starting points for many in making their prayer really come to life. Some Christian traditions with a very heavy emphasis on the Bible find this hard to accept but if individuals can experience new insight from their own growth in prayer through the use of symbols and visual images, they may be emboldened to encourage others to explore these paths as well. God is big enough to be able to teach us in ways other than through the Bible.

The remainder of each morning is devoted to experiential learning.

I am quite sure that the best possible training we can have is to grow in attentiveness to our own spiritual journey, and to what is happening in our work with other people in theirs. There is a kind of triple awareness when we are working at our best with other people – firstly an awareness of the presence of God in the relationship and around us, secondly an awareness of the other person and of their feelings, and thirdly, an awareness of our own feelings in response to what the directee is saying. Without this sensitivity about our own feelings, our own personal bias and prejudices may well colour the relationship. Our own responses are not to be shared in a self-indulgent way, but only if they are likely to help the directee – e.g. 'I'm wondering just why what you are saying is making me feel a bit angry.'

I have outlined below some of the exercises we have found helpful in our morning sessions. This material could possibly be used in one-off groups and meetings as well as longer courses.

Exercises in direction

1) Groups of three or four discuss their own experience of being directed, being asked to stay with their own experience and not to generalize. In a subsequent plenary session

notes are compared and the implications for our own work of direction are drawn out, in particular we try to assess whether people feel there are boundaries to the work of direction.

2) Course members work alone, making notes, on the question 'Where am I now in my own journey?', and then in confidence share with one other member of the course – each being allowed an equal amount of time as talker and listener. In the succeeding plenary session confidences are not broken, but the more general question is asked, 'What did that feel like?'.

3) When twosome sessions take place it is important to ask course members to pair up with a different person each time, so that even within the course they experience a variety of personality. In this exercise we enact the first session of director with directee – the exploratory, setting-up session, allowing half an hour each way, with a short period at the close for the two to discuss how it felt. A closing plenary session is helpful, not to betray any confidences, but to look in more general terms at the kind of issues which occurred most frequently, and what were the main anxieties of those taking the role of director.

Awareness of God's activity

4) A great deal of stress has been laid throughout this book on the *immediacy* of God. Members are sent away with pen and paper and the following question, 'Where and how do you perceive God to have been at work in you and around you in the past seven days or so, and in particular in the past twenty-four hours? Are there any implications for action arising from this awareness?' There will often be a temptation to distance God, or to run away from focusing on one's own journey. This is then shared in twos, in the roles of directee and director, exchanging roles half way. In the concluding plenary discussion there will often emerge widely differing understandings of the extent to which God is involved in the patterns of daily life.

Listening

5) Being a good listener is imperative, and under this heading I would include being a good *watcher*, being able to pick up

non-verbal messages through manner and body language. A very simple early exercise is to break up the group into threes, and for one person to talk for five minutes on any convenient topic, with the other two briefed deliberately to pay as little attention as possible to what is being said. Another member of the three then talks to the other two for five minutes, with the listeners briefed to be *over*-attentive to the speaker. Discussion follows in threes and in plenary on what it felt like to fight against inattentiveness, and how equally alarming was over-concern.

Encouraging others to talk

6) On any course, even given selection, we find that some members come with a considerable case-load of directees – people naturally seem to come to them to talk. Other members may have only one or two people coming to them. We have found it useful to try and help course members to understand a little more about what may be encouraging or inhibiting others from coming to talk to them. This and the following exercise may be useful.

Members are sent off in groups of three or four to consider the following questions (it is assumed that all course members will already have a spiritual director):

(a) What prompted you to contact your spiritual director in the first place?

(b) Did you know whether he/she was a spiritual director already?

(c) How frank and open can you be in that relationship? Are there any areas you feel you cannot discuss?

(d) Do you feel your director is sufficiently objective and able to speak hard truths in love?

(e) Can you identify what it is that encourages you to share things and what it is that discourages you from sharing things you feel to be deeply personal?

A plenary session will help to isolate some of the most salient and frequently repeated points.

'Party conversation'

7) We may not like it, but whether or not people feel able to come and talk with us may well depend on how we field things thrown at us in quite informal situations. A fiercely

judgemental response is not always wrong, but there may be hidden factors behind even quite outrageous statements. 'What awful parties you must go to,' was one response to an exercise we light-heartedly called 'party conversation'!

Six members of the course are handed a slip of paper with a remark on it. In turn they address their question to a chosen member of the group. To avoid embarrassment, the person to whom the remark is addressed is free to give a deliberately insensitive answer if they feel they cannot cope, though in practice most members tend to try to give the best answer they can. The given response and alternative responses are then discussed by the whole group before going on to the next questions. The following are some sample possibilities:

(a) (Said aggressively) 'My sister/brother has been in hospital in a coma ever since a drunken driver ran over her/him nearly a year ago.'

(b) (Also said aggressively, to the Vicar) 'Mary/John (now 8 years old) doesn't want to come to Sunday School any more.'

(c) 'I come to Church every Sunday and I like to think I'm a Christian, but I don't really believe there's anything after this life.'

(d) 'I've given up praying, because none of the things I ask for ever seem to happen.'

(e) 'My firm has agreed on a policy of selling at below-cost prices in the last remaining areas where we have real competition. Soon we shall have eliminated the competition as they are only a small firm.'

(f) 'If they'd just get off their fat backsides they could find a job to do and you and I wouldn't have to pay them unemployment benefit.'

Journalling

8) Journalling has infinite possibilities. Course members go off alone armed with pen and paper and are invited to write freely in confidence:

(a) On a 24 hour clock, what time is it in your life and why?

(b) It is too late to . . .

(c) It is too soon to . . .

(d) Now is the time to . . .

(e) Where is God in this?

Members then form into small groups to discuss how the exercise felt, but are free to share only as much of what they have written as they wish. This is another approach to working on the closeness and reality of God.

9) We have drawn on Ira Progoff as a starting point for this and the following exercise in journalling:

(a) List eight possible paths you might have taken in your life which you did not take.

(b) In one sentence, how do you feel about each of them now?

(c) Can you perceive God at work in those situations?

(d) Expand on one of them.

10) (a) List four possible spiritual paths you might have taken but have not so far taken (e.g. kinds of prayer, reading, study, worship, Christian service, confession, retreats, spiritual direction, etc.).

(b) What do you feel about each of these now, and might the time have now come to explore one or more of them?

Difficulties in prayer and belief

11) The differences between our own and other people's spiritual paths is a recurring theme. We aim at trying to avoid imposing our own pattern on entirely different kinds of personality. Members are divided into groups of four and invited to share their own difficulties in prayer and belief (n.b., their own and not anyone else's), and to respond as helpfully as they can to what other members of the group present.

In the next section of the exercise the foursomes are asked to discuss how helpful or otherwise the responses have been to their own difficulties as presented. A plenary session will then help to make clear which are some of the more common difficulties. On another occasion, attention can be given in a similar way to things that have been found rewarding and helpful in prayer.

Case discussion

12) Apart from our own spiritual path the other all-important raw material for the course is the work which members are

already doing and in which they need support or additional insight. Given due regard to confidentiality and anonymity, members are repeatedly provided with the opportunity to present their work to the group. This may be done either as a straight account, or in the more dramatic form of inviting a group member to 'come as your directee' in role play. When we do this the member who has a case to present in the role of the directee is invited to choose his or her own 'director' from among the others on the course. The chosen 'director' is free to accept or to reject the role. It is always made clear that either 'director' or 'directee' may call a halt to the role play at any time if it is getting too difficult to handle. At whatever point the role play ends, the whole group is then invited to join in discussing the case, but it is always valuable to begin by asking 'director' and 'directee' for their responses to the experience.

I have made it clear from the start that since the courses have no resident guru, they will to some extent be self-programming. Accordingly after lunch there is always a half-hour session on administration, when the group agrees what topics it would be helpful to pursue, particularly the topics for the more 'head-learning' afternoon sessions. Should there be time left over, this is given to discussion of any more general points or problems which course members may wish to raise.

The afternoons are usually, but not always, fairly straight lectures followed by discussion. Our modest course fees enable us to pay a small sum to visiting speakers, but such has been the calibre of those attending our course that on a number of occasions we have had the pleasure of being lectured to by our own members. Because the afternoon topics are agreed by the course, it follows that the programme varies widely from year to year.

Counselling in earlier years tended to devalue the importance of spiritual direction and 'God-talk', so in the first year of our course we aim to give course members confidence in *using* the language of theology when appropriate, and only in the second year to reinforce some of the psychological insights which many of them already possess. I think it is most important that Spiritual Direction is seen as a valued discipline in its own right.

Here are some of the themes which have emerged for the

afternoon sessions, for which we have either used our own resources, or, more frequently, engaged outside speakers:

Spiritual Direction and the Biblical Tradition
The Desert Fathers
The Benedictine Tradition
The Franciscan Tradition
The Orthodox Tradition
The Ignatian Tradition
Caroline Spirituality
Charles de Foucauld
Peasant Spirituality and Popular Religion
Charismatic Spirituality
Evangelical Spirituality
The Spirituality of the Work-place
Religious Experience
Developing the Ministry of Direction
Myers-Briggs and Spiritual Paths
The Mid-Life Crisis
The Direction Relationship
Transference
Male and Female in Direction
The Shadow
Dreams
Dependency in Direction
Spiritual Direction and Ethics

The calibre of members has been, almost without exception, outstandingly high. As already explained, we have insisted that those who come should be involved in directing others and themselves be being directed. Numbers of applicants have grown, however, to such an extent, that in future there will have to be some kind of interviewing, so that places can be given to those most likely to benefit from the training. Originally I had envisaged ten to twelve members, but in the first two years we eventually extended to sixteen. Despite a high commitment to the course, unavoidable absences mean that we usually find ourselves as a group of twelve, which is ideal both for plenary work and for smaller groupings.

We have not been unaware that a daytime course limits those who can attend (though we have in both years had the benefit of a more or less balanced number of women and men), and preliminary soundings have encouraged me to set up an additional evening course, which will meet fortnightly but take two years to cover the ground covered in a year by the daytime course.

Originally, I had intended that the one-year course should stand on its own as complete in itself, while also offering the possibility of a second, individually tailored year which could help those who so wished to find ways of exploring whatever aspect of direction or spirituality each found most helpful – whether by following one particular tradition, developing counselling skills, or exploring Myers-Briggs or journalling or whatever. For those who wished to continue still further, a third year could concentrate wholly on work supervision (with due regard to confidentiality).

In the event, it became clear that one year of general training was insufficient, and a great deal was still to be done; so the second year has become 'more of the same', enabling a further growing together of the group and therefore a still more open sharing and learning in depth. The course ends with the conclusion of the second year, with the option of an ongoing monthly support group for case-discussion into the third year.

How have we financed the course? It runs on a shoestring budget: meetings are in my house; we had an initial £200 grant from the Diocese to get us going and a charity provided us with a further £200. Course members contribute £5 a term (to be increased to £7), primarily to pay a small honorarium to visiting speakers but also to cover a not inconsiderable amount of postage and stationery. We have also begun to build up a small lending library, because many of the most useful books are published in the United States, and rather expensive for individual course members to buy.

Some people argue that greater financial commitment makes for greater course commitment. This may be true in some instances, but we have found commitment to our courses to be good. I have a deeper concern, too, for not charging large sums of money for the course unless absolutely necessary: many things that happen in church life today have come to Britain from the United States, but here we do not have the same amount of money to spare, and in no way could many American ventures take place in Third World countries. I feel strongly that wherever it can (though this is politically unfashionable), the Church should set an example of laying on its training as inexpensively as possible, and as far as possible on a voluntary basis. All too many dioceses are extending their paid specialist staff by leaps and bounds. I am convinced that in many instances such work can still be done effectively, not by paid diocesan 'experts', who do not have the responsibility of a parish, but by parochial clergy and others learning to specialize in one area or another. This could save parishes a considerable amount of the quota which dioceses would have to spend for full-time 'experts'. Most parochial clergy enjoy and derive benefit from extra-parochial work, and will do it 'for free'! This system is also more easily copied by countries less well off than ourselves. I have long held that everyone in full-time parish employment should have at least one area of interest and specialization outside the parish, and the amount of time I have been spending on SPIDIR courses, as well as on the direction of a considerable number of clergy and others from outside the parish, does not seem to have encroached unduly on the time available for running the parish itself.

I hope that our experience in Southwark may encourage others to set up courses in Spiritual Direction, and I should be very grateful to have any information available about what is happening elsewhere. This is a comparatively new field of training and we all need to help each other.

The following is a summary of our aims and objectives.

SPIDIR courses in spiritual direction

Overall aim

The purpose of the course is that members should grow in confidence in the practice of spiritual direction.

Objectives of first year course

That members should:
1) Become more familiar with some of the major historical traditions of spirituality and direction.
2) Become more aware of God and their own spiritual needs.
3) Through group methods, prayer and subsequent discussion, become more sensitive to the differing needs and responses of others.

Objectives of second year course

That members should:

1) Understand more fully aspects of the direction relationship.
2) Be helped to extend their own ministry of direction.
3) Understand the need for continuing support and be helped towards finding this.

The course is open to anyone, lay or ordained, who finds that people come to them to talk about their faith in relation to prayer and everyday life.

10 Spiritual Direction and Parish Strategy

It will be clear by now that I am convinced that spiritual direction should play a far more central and important part in parish life than it has in recent years. Obviously it would be absurd to expect that all clergy will wish, or even are able, to make spiritual direction a high personal priority. Mercifully the Anglican Church in England is still broad enough for a wide variety of personal styles of ministry to coexist, and long may it so remain. Nevertheless, where the clergy in a parish do not see spiritual direction as their own personal path, they will probably be able to spot one or two lay members of the congregation with the potential gifts for this ministry.

Kenneth Leech, in his recent *Spirituality and Pastoral Care*[1], has argued cogently in general terms for the need to reinstate spiritual direction at the heart of pastoral strategy. This chapter is concerned with fleshing out that general point of view in terms of personal parochial experience.

In the lush ecclesiastical days around 1960, when I was at theological college, every week visiting speakers used to come to lecture on their pet subjects (which never included spiritual direction). Their offerings were subsequently praised or pulled to pieces over the lunch or supper table. On only two occasions in two years can I recall universal agreement that the visitor was good.

One of these two acclaimed visitors was a much respected parish priest who came to offer his 'Plan for the Parish', a comprehensive scheme involving the creation of a multitude of organizations for every age-group and every kind of person in the parish.

Some years later it happened that I found myself incumbent of that same parish where our visitor had hammered out his ideas and put them into practice.

The scheme provided womb-to-tomb care. From post-baptismal visiting, through mothers'-and-toddlers' clubs, into crèches, Sunday schools, uniformed organizations, junior, middle and senior youth clubs (both closed and open), organizations for the 18–30 age range, men's groups, women's groups, and so on and on. Nothing was left out. It was as though the parish organization was like a bucket, with parishioners as the water inside just waiting to find a way of escape, so that unless every possible hole was plugged with yet another organization, they would leak out of the bucket and be lost for ever. It felt like a desperate maintenance operation to keep the water inside the bucket.

When I arrived in the parish there had been two intervening incumbents, but with the experience of a difficult but exciting Inner City first incumbency behind me I was convinced that their predecessor's 'Plan for the Parish' could be in some measure reinstated. In all fairness it should be said that over a seven-year period our communicant numbers increased by no less than 90%, but deep down I think I realized from the start that for me at least it was not really the best way to run a parish. I knew it would not have worked in my Inner City parish, and I knew it would not work in smaller country parishes, in neither of which would there be enough people to staff or even belong to such a vast range of activities and organizations. It was essentially a strategy for a suburban or commuter-belt parish. I was often painfully aware, too, that I was spending so much time in finding, supporting and supervising leaders, and in mopping up leaders who felt inadequate or wanted to quit, that there was virtually no time for any one-to-one work helping people to grow as Christians or ponder their ministry from the standpoint of where they were themselves. Everything seemed to take second place to a predetermined pattern of organizations. Indeed, I had made a policy decision before starting in that parish, that the population was too large for me to work on a one-to-one basis, and the only effective way to run things was by finding and supporting lay leaders to do the more immediate contact with others. It seemed a reasonable and plausible strategy for a large parish – yet I was increasingly uneasy.

My unease was shared by others, and one day someone asked me why I spent so much of my time organizing and reorganizing people and neglecting what they felt was some kind of a capacity for one-to-one work. Only a few days later a good friend in the parish handed me a copy of a well known quotation from Petronius Arbiter, written in 210 BC:

> We trained hard, but it seemed that every time we were
> beginning to form up into teams we would be reorganized. I

was to learn later in life that we tend to meet any new situations by reorganizing: and a wonderful method it can be for creating the illusion of progress while producing confusion, inefficiency and demoralization.

My friend had intended the reference to apply to our diocesan Pastoral Committee, which was then in the throes of yet another cry of 'Wolf', with threats of dire pastoral reorganization throughout the diocese, but I could not help feeling there was an application nearer home.

My time in that parish was coming to an end, and it was too late to make any major change of direction there, but I knew it would be important to rethink my basic parish strategy when I moved to a new one. Nowadays I often have a feeling of *déjà vu*, as I visit different churches, and find myself confronted by a notice sheet or magazine, or hear the notices at a service, listing a vast range of endless and almost neurotic *activity*. It is like being back in my old parish – clubs, organizations, meetings, societies, services every morning, afternoon and evening, seven days a week. The list leaves me with a sense of total exhaustion without even beginning to participate in the week's events.

A highly organized parish not only induces in some of us that sense of fatigue: it attempts to tie up its key members in an endless round of organizations and administration. Even worse, it all too easily enwraps people in a claustrophobic web of 'churchiness'. Where, one asks, are the opportunities for people to talk quietly about what is happening in their work, where a Christian point of view might well affect important decisions? Church members, once they get home from work, all too easily become trapped in a round of churchy activities which seldom gear in with their Monday-to-Friday, 9-to-5 world.

Over the years I have encountered a fair number of once-active church people who on moving to a new area lie very low because they do not wish to be caught up once more in an exhausting treadmill of parish activities, leaving little time for family life or the cultivation of friendships and hobbies, let alone the peace and quiet needed to develop a mature prayer life. Parish activity can easily become an alternative world in which people escape from reality. No wonder, then, that the psychologically damaged want to take refuge in it, while the healthy simply do not want to know.

I am not saying that a parish should attempt to function without organizations at all – some are essential and others are valuable. But I do not think we should collapse in despair should our own Christian community not be able to provide a water-tight range of organizations and groups.

One needs only to look a little way back into the Christian past to realize that, for century after century, Christian life was maintained and handed down without the endless frenetic activity which seems to be the order of the day in today's 'successful' parish. No village community could provide either leaders or members for so comprehensive a round of parish organizations, and yet the Christian Way has flourished and developed without this compulsive activity.

Let us, rather, take for our starting point, not the 'successful' commuter belt area, but the Inner City parish or the smaller suburban or village area, and see whether what we have dis-cussed in the area of spiritual direction might not provide a model for parishes which do not attempt to set up a second, alternative, escapist world in opposition to the 'real' world of work and politics and international affairs. I am not denying that many 'successful' and busy parishes include within them im-portant prayer and Bible study groups, and outreach activities which do get to grips with the 'real' world. It is ultimately not so much an either/or situation, as a question of where we start, of what are our basic aims and our general direction. Is ministry to the parish something imposed from above in a series of groups and organizations which people are asked to join or to lead, or is it better expressed in learning how to release gifts and poten-tialities dormant within our members? Once those potentialities are realized, Christians can choose to exercise their gifts accord-ing to their own inner dynamic.

Let us then assume, for the moment, a parish structure which holds as its primary focus the basic Sunday worship, but which then encourages as many members of the congregation as possible to be bold enough to come to talk with someone two, three or four times a year, about how they are getting on in their Christian journey, and especially about how their prayer life is going, along the lines discussed in this book.

As they grow – and they *will* grow – not only will they be able to relate their prayer and belief more closely to their working and family life and to their political allegiance (which are the

96

primary areas of their potential Christian effectiveness); they will also have their own newly released gifts to apply to the life of the Church. Prayer groups and courses will spring from people's real needs rather than from the Vicar's latest bright idea. Those with gifts to offer will be able to use them according to their own enthusiasm, which is more likely to be infectious than trying to fit into someone else's grand parish strategy.

With a reduced level of activity within the parish there will be more time for prayer, for real meeting, for talking about the things that really matter. Clergy may find themselves less in control, but acting far more as 'enablers' who help to release the God-given potential already existing within their members.

In many respects, to give priority to one-to-one work is to return to a much earlier concept of parochial ministry, going back beyond the nineteenth and twentieth century obsession with organizations and with busy-ness. One-to-one work shows that people *matter as individuals*, and although very time-consuming, unlike counselling it does not require any long-drawn-out weekly commitment to particular individuals. It may well be that the disproportionate amount of time needed for counselling has in recent years blinded many to the fact that we can 'hold' quite a lot of people if we are talking to them only three or four times a year.

I realize that I may have painted a very black and white, 'either/or' picture in this chapter. Nevertheless, I think that an important shift of emphasis could usefully be made towards spending more time with individuals, despite the fact that for quite a while it may seem as though not much is happening. It is not necessarily an elitist stance to hold that growth in depth may be considerably more important than growth in numbers.

Once a fair proportion of the members of a congregation have discovered through their one-to-one sessions that they can really talk about God and the world, about their own prayer life and relationship with God, discussion in groups will become easier, and talk among Christian friends will be able more readily to go below the superficial.

However, it does need careful planning to develop this sort of strategy, which is more easily initiated by a new incumbent on moving to a fresh parish than mid-term in a ministry.

It is much easier on beginning in a new parish to make it clear, through preaching, talking and in magazine articles, that one *expects* to talk with people about prayer, that one *expects* people will come to talk about the things that matter, and that there is plenty of time for this. I always make it clear when anyone comes to talk that we have a whole hour if we want it. A School of Prayer can helpfully be laid on quite soon after arrival, and soundings made about the extent of people's readiness for an ongoing prayer group.

Like many clergy I have made a point of delivering a circular get-to-know-you letter to every house in the parish on arrival, which also stresses my readiness to talk about things that matter. The value of this operation is beyond doubt; people have referred to it with appreciation even years later.

It quite quickly gets round that one is not prepared to drink cups of tea and talk about the weather, but never too busy to talk about God. I was not entirely displeased to hear it said on one occasion that the only thing I seemed to be interested in was prayer. For some people it came as a shock a little later to realize that prayer was inescapably linked with politics and international affairs.

Stewardship campaign leaflets should, I am sure, always contain a box headed something like, 'Would you like to talk with one of us about how you are getting on?' Unexpected and encouraging responses invariably result.

There is always a danger in enthusiasms going over the edge and claiming too much. As I have suggested earlier, the Parish Communion was once thought to be the answer to all the ills of the Church, then Christian Stewardship was seen as the great way to bring the Church to life again. More recently there have been those who have believed that everything is done best in small groups – or that what the Church most needs is management skills – or work supervision or parish audits. I suspect the current enthusiasm is for experiential learning, with little but contempt for 'head' and academic learning.

The danger is that if too much is claimed for a new enthusiasm, disillusion will set in and a valuable tool will become undervalued, when the truth is that those I have mentioned, and many more, do have a limited but real value when used rightly. It would be sad if the current enthusiasm for spiritual direction should claim too much for itself, and result in another round of disillusion.

But I do not think that spiritual direction *will* go this way. It closely resembles Christian Healing. Both spiritual direction and Christian Healing are time-honoured and traditional parts of the Christian ministry, which over the years have been sadly neglected. They are not new paths; what we are seeing is a recovery of what has been lost, which is therefore less susceptible to rapid changes in ecclesiastical fashion.

Even more importantly – and here I return to where I began: in true spiritual direction, the real director is the Holy Spirit. The human 'director' has a marginal existence somewhat resembling John the Baptist's role: 'He must increase; I must decrease.' It is a role which calls for a great deal of humility, and is therefore not an easy one for a parish priest with a compulsion towards massive organization or empire-building or imagined 'promotion'. Those 999 out of 1,000 spiritual directors deplored by St John of the Cross were probably too authoritarian, too directive, too concerned about their own power over others, about their own ecclesiastical careers, instead of trying to be inconspicuous channels for the working of the Holy Spirit.

Yet somewhere, even within the most organized set-up, there will be a few who are ready to sit down and listen both to the other person and to the promptings of the Holy Spirit – the true director.

It is because I trust in the power of the Holy Spirit that I believe the current enthusiasm for spiritual direction is not just another passing fashion which will once more fade out into a relatively insignificant role. Rather, I see spiritual direction as an enduring front-line weapon, so effective that it can become one of the most important strategies of parochial ministry.

Notes

1: Elitism or a path for all?

1. Leech, Kenneth, *Soul Friend* (Sheldon Press 1977).
   —— *True God* (Sheldon Press 1985).
   —— *Spirituality and Pastoral Care* (Sheldon Press 1986).
   Bryant, Christopher, *The River Within* (Darton, Longman and Todd 1973).
   —— *The Heart in Pilgrimage* (Darton, Longman and Todd 1980).
   —— *Jung and the Christian Way* (Darton, Longman and Todd 1983).
2. Barry, W. A., and Connolly, W. J. *The Practice of Spiritual Direction* (New York, Seabury Press, 1982), p. 9.
3. Thornton, Martin, *Spiritual Direction* (SPCK 1984).
4. Merton, Thomas, *Spiritual Direction and Meditation* (Anthony Clarke 1950), pp. 20–5.

2: What are people's needs?

1. Hurding, Roger, *Roots and Shoots* (Hodder and Stoughton 1985).

3: Patterns of direction

1. Thornton, Martin, *Spiritual Direction* (SPCK 1984).
2. Barry, W. A., and Connolly, W. J. *The Practice of Spiritual Direction* (New York, Seabury Press, 1982).
3. Clinebell, Howard, *Basic Types of Pastoral Care and Counselling* (SCM Press 1984), pp. 31–4.
4. Hurding, Roger, *Roots and Shoots* (Hodder and Stoughton 1986), p. 226.

4: The first session

1. Devers, Dorothy, *Faithful Friendship*. (Privately printed. Obtained through Church of the Savior bookshop, Washington DC.)

5: The ongoing task

1. I regret that I have not been able to trace the source(s) of these two quotations.
2. May, Gerald, *Care of Mind, Care of Spirit* (New York, Harper and Row, 1982).
   —— *Will and Spirit* (New York, Harper and Row, 1982).
3. Ellis, Albert, *Reason and Emotion in Psychotherapy* (New Jersey, Citadel Press, 1979).

6: Resources in direction

1. John 16.12.
2. Wink, Walter, *Transforming Bible Study* (SCM Press 1980).

3. Elliott, Charles, *Praying the Kingdom* (Darton, Longman and Todd 1985).
4. Progoff, Ira, *At a Journal Workshop* (New York, Dialogue House Library, 1980).
   —— *The Practice of Process Meditation* (New York, Dialogue House Library, 1980).
5. Emmaus House, Clifton Hill, Clifton, Bristol, BS8 4PD.
6. Kiersey, David, and Bates, Marilyn, *Please Understand Me* (California, Prometheus Nemesis Book Company, 1984), p. 5.
7. Briggs-Myers, Isabel, *Gifts Differing* (California, Consulting Psychologists Press, 1980), chaps. 9, 16.
8. Chester, Michael P. and Norrisey, Marie C., *Prayer and Temperament* (Charlottesville, The Open Door, 1984). Obtainable from St Paul Book Centre, Kensington High Street, London, W8.

7: The place of the retreat in spiritual direction

1. Information about these retreats is available from the Revd Peter Dodson, Retreats Promotion Centre, St Martin-Le-Grand, Coney Street, YORK, YO1 1QL.

8: Direction and the 'outsider'

1. Bailey, Edward (ed.), *Breakthrough, a Work Book in Popular Religion* (Partners Publications, 17, Edward Road, Dorset, DT1 2HL, 1986).
2. Edwards, Tilden, *Spiritual Friend* (New York, Paulist Press, 1980).

9. Training the directors

1. Quoted in Hurding, Roger, *Roots and Shoots* (Hodder and Stoughton 1985), pp. 311–12.
2. Edwards, Tilden, *Spiritual Friend* (New York, Paulist Press, 1980), p. 108.
3. £1.00 sent to Cora Lindley, 25 Crichton Road, Carshalton Beeches, Surrey, will obtain copies for a year.
4. Di Mello, Anthony, *Sadhana* (Anand, India, Gujarat Sahitya Prakash, 1978).
5. Di Mello, Anthony, *Wellsprings* (Anand, India, Gujarat Sahitya Prakash, 1984).
6. Kroll, Una, *The Spiritual Exercise Book* (Firethorn Press 1985).

10: Spiritual direction and parish strategy

1. Leech, Kenneth, *Spirituality and Pastoral Care* (Sheldon Press 1986).

Postscript

This book will have served its purpose if it helps the reader either to find a spiritual friend or director, or to have the courage to *be* a spiritual friend to a few others, or even just to read and talk more widely on the subject.

For those already experienced in direction, for whom this book may have had little new to say, perhaps our S P I D I R experience may encourage them to set up similar opportunities to help others to grow in this ministry. I should be very grateful to hear of any such ventures, so as to be able to record how this kind of training is developing, with a view to possible wider sharing of experiences and insights.

St Anselm's House
43 Ham Common
Richmond-upon-Thames
Surrey
February 1987   TW10 7JH

Index

Index

Praying the Kingdom
  (Elliot) 49
'privatized'
  Christianity 40
Progoff, Ira 50–1, 87
psychological
  problems 19–20

quiet days 56–7

reading 55
relationships 13–14, 27,
  30–1, 45, 55, 72–3,
  75–6
relaxation 56
resistance to God 43–4
retreats 56–7; 'client-
  centred' 62–7;
  Fellowship of
  Contemplative
  Prayer 61; home-
  based 63–6;
  Ignatian 61–3;

themes 66–7
role play 88
Roots and Shoots
  (Hurding) 12, 22, 76

sacraments 57
saints, calendar of 46
sensitivity 16
service 43, 58
setting for sessions 27
silence 29
society, adjustment to 23
Soul Friend (Leech) 22–3
SPIDIR 9, 68, 74, 78–92
Spiritual Direction
  (Thornton) 3, 15–16
spiritual friendship 29
*Spirituality and Pastoral
  Care* (Leech) 93
stocktaking 5–6

tertiaries 58
Thornton, Martin 3,

15–16, 82
time-limit on
  sessions 27–8
training 78–92; aims and
  objectives 91–2;
  courses 81–92;
  finance 90–1; SPIDIR
  network 78–81;
  topics 80, 88–9
Transforming Bible Study
  (Wink) 45

variety of ways to
  God 15–16

wants 31–2
Way of a Pilgrim, The
  (anon.) 10–11
work 20–1, 58–9, 65
worship, corporate 47–8

Yoga 59–60